I Am NOT My THOUGHTS

Thoughts *rule your life until you get the revelation:* ***they*** *are not* ***you****.*

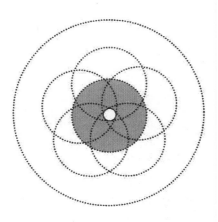

Dick Dalton, Ph.D.

Don't miss the Preface and Introduction!

The Table of Contents

I am an Individual:

a unique, indivisible being (person, soul, entity)
connected energetically to all that exists.
I have a body, thoughts,
feelings, relationships, and spirit.
I do observe when I'm *awake* (aware)
and make decisions when given a choice.
I follow through when
I exercise my power of will.

Strategies for Intentional Living

1. Determine from your yearnings a goal or project.
2. Discern your allies & your obstacles along the way.
3. Decide that you **are** the one that **can** & **will** do this.
4. Dig for more understanding by asking questions.
5. Don't give up on this possibility of a better world.

If it is to be, it is up to US!

Do YOU ever do things
YOU don't want to do?

Which Y*OU* is you?

Preface

Do you ever do things you don't want to do? This book is for you. Still waiting to be happy, healthy, have peace of mind, feel secure, and/or love and be loved? This book is for you. You've known or heard about me and are just curious about my first book? I trust you won't be disappointed.

This is a book about thoughts. You and I are thinking and we're pretty sure all humans have had thoughts for a good portion of their short stay here. Are **you** your thoughts? Do thoughts control you or do you control your thoughts? What are **thoughts**, anyway?

One of my seasoned psychology professors at Mizzou in the 1970s answered my question with, "We don't talk about **thoughts** because we can't measure them." I was amazed! What is psychology then? Merriam-Webster defines psychology as "the science of <u>mind</u> and behavior." It says <u>mind</u> "is the part of a person that **thinks**" and 'thought' is "an idea…the act or process of **thinking**." As recent as Feb. 2012, Ezequiel Morsella PhD said in "What is a Thought" (*Psychology Today*), "What thoughts are remains mysterious from a neuroscientific point of view."

I am boldly calling this a true psychology book; possibly an important one because it is all about 'measuring' thoughts and thinking. In keeping with "the science of mind," I need a hypothesis:

> If people come to understand they are NOT their thoughts, but have been controlled by their powerful subconscious thoughts and the thoughts of others; **then** the probability increases that they will take more control over their own thoughts and actions and significantly increase their discernment, compassion, inner peace, and love.

This is also a philosophy book. Word. "**Philosophy**: the study of ideas about knowledge, truth, the nature and meaning of life, etc." This is definitely a philosophy book. In this genre, you'll find discussions on identity, values, ethics, control, cause, and *God*. See Page 59 for why I italicize the term *God*.

Some might go so far as to say this is a **theology** book. Word. "Theology is the study of religious faith, beliefs, practice and experience." The book is not promoting any religion, but 'cherry picks' some of the wisdom of many religious cultures including the Bible—all in support of the premise: I am NOT my Thoughts. [See Chapter 1, We see the world through our beliefs.]

According to the artist Ian Milliss, **I am an artist** and **this is an art book**. I love his quote reproduced in ***Identity & Anonymity***, edited by Jonathan Talbot, Leslie Fandrich, and Steven M. Specht (2016). Notice the word ***memes***.

> "I would say that the artist's role
> is to generate a stream of ideas
> that helps human society to constantly adapt,
> to create and modify the cultural memes
> that underlie our behavior and production."

Taking it a step further, **I am a Social Artist**. [See Page 182] As a painter works with paints on a canvass, a Social Artist works with the ***memes*** (cultural values and ideas) of individuals and groups to bring about the emergence of the beautiful. Chapter 11, Can you find your Self?, gives understanding and exercises related to Social Artistry.

Humans communicate through symbols. "CAT" is the symbolic arrangement of abstract letters referring to *you know what*. Language uses agreed upon symbols to communicate—send and receive messages. In my college speech class, this was referred to as **Social Intercourse**. Chapter 8, Do you have any Misconceptions?, takes you through my own presentation of this important analogy in my college **Personal and Community Health** classes.

I use this analogy of social intercourse in separating you, the individual, from your thoughts. For some of you, it may be a hard sell. I would only request your own self-examination of the ***memes*** you now agree with that rise up to compete with what I am presenting. When did you acquire your beliefs? See Chapter 3, You are the Gardener.

I use the term *memes* (rhymes with dreams) throughout the book. *Memes* are packets of cultural (social) information passed on from mind to mind through communication (social intercourse). Richard Dawkins coined the term *meme* in 1976 while writing *The Selfish Gene*. He was looking for an analogy to genes. Genes are physical packets of information passed from generation to generation through sexual intercourse.

Cultural information (*memes*) includes history, art work, imaginations, plans, music, politics, religion, philosophy and all the other realms of knowledge and activities, including psychology. All our relationships are embedded in the values of various cultures and sub-cultures of our society and family. We transmit these cultures by our *memes*.

Much of this transmission of culture is automatic (some say robotic). We transmit to others somewhat like it was transmitted to us. This is how cultural values have been so influential in the repetition of 'mistakes' of the past. We received our earliest *memes* in a unique context with little to no filters to sort the healthy from the unhealthy. We took the *memes* in and most of them stuck. We became new messengers of the old culture and co-creators of the new culture.

The curious thing about *memes* is they are always mutating and mixing with other *memes* as we encounter unique situations. We talk about fusion food and fusion music. *Memes* have been the **masters of fusion** since their beginning. We could also say they are the **masters of confusion** for the same reason.

Society does not like to think they are slaves of a master. Society likes to hold up the *memes* of **personal responsibility** and **free will** as though everyone has always had them. I contend up front that **our will is never free.** We each have a will, but it is constantly influenced, limited, and/or manipulated by the powers of competing *memes* inside and outside each mind. See Chapter 4, Who is Driving your Car?

You're familiar with cartoons (or **Animal House**) that have depicted mythical competing *memes* as the 'good angel' on one shoulder and the 'devil' on the other shoulder. Most people see the point of the cartoon; but when the comedian, Flip Wilson, used the phrase, "The devil made me do it," another *meme* said, "The devil can't make anyone do anything because everyone has free will." Many 'free will' advocates may also say they sin a little bit every day (because of the devil). The *meme wars* continue. See Chapter 15 (Meme Wars).

Mental Slavery is the norm in our world. So teachers admonish their students, *"Take control of your own mind."* First, you must become aware of what's in your mind and what it means to be a **mental slave.** The well-known humanistic philosopher, Erich Fromm, states in his book, *The Art of Being,*

> ... Man can be a slave even without being put in chains...
> The outer chains have simply been put inside of man.
> The desires and thoughts that the suggestion apparatus
> of society fills him with, chain him more thoroughly
> than outer chains.
> This is so because man can at least be aware of outer chains
> but be unaware of inner chains,
> carrying them with the illusion that he is free.
> He can try to overthrow the outer chains,
> but how can he rid himself of chains of whose existence
> he is unaware?

This powerful and revealing statement applies to all of us in our early years and, for many, this mental slavery continues throughout the lifespan. Paradoxically, it sometimes feels easier to be a mental slave than to do the difficult work of releasing yourself from the mental chains. See Chapter 10, Stress is Too Much!

On May 18, 2016, my letter to the editor was published in *The Jefferson City News Tribune.*

I Am NOT My Thoughts!

Dear Editor,

   While singing with the Monticello men at our annual Memorial Day concert in the Rotunda last year, I was struck by one of the quotes etched there in huge letters: "IDEAS CONTROL THE WORLD." It does not say *God* controls or government controls or, for that matter, the devil controls the world.

   During my 25 years as a non-denominational Christian minister, I became keenly aware that each individual has a unique way of perceiving the world, issues in the world, *God*, who's right, and who's wrong. This should not be surprising since we each grow up having unique experiences. Even identical twins that start out with the very same genes grow more and more different genetically as they age due to their different experiences.

   Our ideas and beliefs get established very young and are sometimes modified by personal experiences. What could possibly get us to change a belief? When our mother's back did not break after we stepped on a crack? Finding out that presents came from our parents could get us to change our belief that a man and a bunch of elves actually live at the North Pole and deliver toys to girls and boys.

   History describes how people changed their belief that the sun revolved around the earth. Now we all accept and believe instead that the earth revolves around the sun. That change was due to certain individuals carefully observing what was going on in the night sky. Those early scientific discoveries challenged the status quo beliefs of the day promoted by the church. Eventually, church leaders and followers changed their beliefs.

   I would like to offer a somewhat new idea: "The world we live in is between our ears." Each of us 'lives in our own world.' We agree to cooperate with those whose world seems more like ours and we 'fight' with those worlds that seem different. Our own ideas control our own little world. It is good to remember that we were not born with these ideas. We all acquired them along the way.

   When we 'fight' each other, it is really ideas that fight ideas and ideas get our bodies to say things and do things even to the point of violence. I believe the Rotunda quote may be right on: "IDEAS CONTROL THE WORLD." How about you?

As I was finalizing this book for printing, my wife and I took a short vacation. Wanting a book to read on the trip, I was surprised to see *Ishmael* by Daniel Quinn (1992) sitting on one of my bookshelves. I have no recollection of how it got there, but I knew many friends had read it back in the 90s and it had become a cult classic. To my further surprise, it included this:

> **Teacher** (p.34): "...it was not only the Jews who were captives under Hitler. The entire German nation was a captive, including his enthusiastic supporters."
> **Student:** "I think I see what you mean."
> **Teacher:** "What was it that held them captive?"

After several guesses by the student, the teacher said that <u>Hitler told them a story</u>, the sad story of what they, as individuals and as a country, had gone through since the end of WWI. He then gave them a vision for how he could **make Germany great again** and "it had an almost overwhelming appeal to the people of Germany."

On Dec.15, 2016, I nearly fell out of my chair reading this:

> **Teacher** (p.252): "There is one significant difference between the inmates of your criminal prisons and the inmates of your <u>cultural prison</u>: The former understand that the distribution of wealth and power inside the prison has nothing to do with justice... In your <u>cultural prison</u>, which inmates wield the power?"
>
> **Student:** "The male inmates. Especially the white male inmates."
>
> **Teacher:** "Yes, that's right. But you understand that these white male inmates are indeed inmates and not warders. For all their power and privilege—for all that they lord it over everyone else in the prison—not one of them has a key that will unlock the gate."
>
> **Student:** "Yes, that's true. <u>Donald Trump</u> can do a lot of things I can't, but he can no more get out of the prison than I can. But what does this have to do with justice?"
>
> **Teacher:** "Justice demands that people other than white males have power in the prison."

Donald Trump was the only non-fictional person mentioned in this 1992 book (other than Hitler) and now Donald Trump has just been elected President of the USA. His cultural status has not changed.

I am NOT my Thoughts is a book for every coach, parent, minister, teacher, counselor, and individual. I have played each of these roles and have seen the power of these ideas help thousands in their journey. The threads of **autobiographical** content are intended as a springboard for you to dig in and get more deeply personal in your own self-examination and inner growth.

My intention throughout this book is to provide a series of **mental mirrors** to give you the opportunity to become aware (or more aware) of the **mental slavery** all experience and offer tested tools for **releasing** yourself and others. As your understanding grows—revelation by revelation—apply the tools. They become more powerful the more you use them.

Introduction

The book started as a set of **parable** cards. "A **parable** is an allegory—a story, poem, or picture that can be interpreted to reveal a hidden meaning; **synonym**: analogy, metaphor, symbol, or emblem." (Online dictionary)

Why does this book title sound both familiar and foreign? The idea is not really new, but you may not have encountered it—at least in this form. I know from my life experience that I was thirty years old before I was actually told, "You are not your thoughts." Do you remember when you first heard those words?

I grew up in a middleclass Methodist home going to public schools, went to two Midwest universities, was in therapy with a psychiatrist for six months for mild depression, finished my bachelor's degree, spent almost four years in the Navy and was discharged from the brig because of depression. I lived on a commune, became a yoga teacher, got married, had a child, had more therapy, and my wife and child moved out. Depression set in again. After a mystical experience in my living room and a series of 'coincidences,' I was guided to a roadside church where I first heard, "You are not your thoughts."

Being told this was an instant relief. The man across the table saw **me** and knew the barrage of depressing thoughts I had just unloaded were NOT **me**. I needed to hear and apply that message for several years before I got the full revelation of what it meant. I began to experience what my hypothesis in the Preface said I would:

> If people come to understand they are NOT their thoughts, but have been controlled by their powerful subconscious thoughts and the thoughts of others; **then** the probability increases that they will take more control over their own thoughts and actions and significantly increase their discernment, compassion, inner peace, and love.

Sitting with the pastor at that roadside church in 1975, I was seeking help (humility) and hungry for answers (asking questions) about why I was so depressed and what I was really supposed to do with my life. As answers were consistently and repeatedly given, my self-love and love of others gradually replaced my fears; my understanding also grew and deepened. Perhaps you have had a similar experience.

In 2001, my wife and I were invited by our blind friend, Wayne Anderson, to the monthly dinner at the Lenoir retirement village. As he and his beautiful guide dog were checking in, he would not allow them to use his dog as an excuse to seat our little group to the side. We then were seated at a round table with four or five other residents of the village. They wore nametags.

One little lady's tag read Thelma McArthur and I said, "I went to high school with Kay McArthur." She said it was her daughter. Another resident's name was McGinity. His two sons were in the same high school class with Kay and me. Marsha and I were invited to visit Thelma at her home. I felt a deep kinship that led to weekly Friday lunches out and extended conversations until her passing over ten years later.

Around 2005 during one of our Friday sessions and thirty years after that first conversation with the pastor in 1975, Thelma introduced me to Roberto Assagioli's book, *The Act of Will*. [Curiously, this wonderful man had died in 1974.] As I scanned through his book, my eyes riveted on the phrase, **"I am not my thoughts."** It was one of a series of phrases I had been using in my classroom for years. I was both excited and humbled.

I have asked a number of folks to recall when they first heard **"You are not your thoughts."** Of the few that remembered **ever** hearing the phrase, most answered, "In counseling." That lets me know this 'secret knowledge' needs to be broadcast far and wide. Those that have 'ears to hear' will come to understand and spread the good news.

I can't know if the images and ideas in this book will excite and humble you. It may have to do with your intention, motivation, and/or level of consciousness. You get to look in your own **mental mirror** for that answer or this book may act as a **mental mirror** for you. Look closely and don't be afraid of what you see. Let love replace your fears and the revelations will start pouring in.

An Exercise to Change Your Life

Roberto Assagioli, the Italian doctor and author of **The Act of Will:** *A Guide to Self-Actualization and Self-Realization* (1974), provides a daily practice that will help change your life significantly. Simply repeat the following phrases and then apply them to situations such as hearing complaining thoughts go through your mind, looking in the mirror at your body, or noticing a kind of 'wrestling match' involving your own thoughts, feelings, relationships, or spirit.

> I have a body, but I am not my body.
>
> I have thoughts, but I am not my thoughts.
>
> I have feelings, but I am not my feelings.
>
> I have relationships, but I am not my relationships.
>
> I have spirit, but I am not my spirit.

Words repeated are a good start, but they are not the same as having a revelation (epiphany, insight). A revelation is the 'ah-ha', the light bulb coming on, the understanding of the words coming alive, the paradigm shift that shifts everything. After a revelation, you don't see yourself or the world in the same way. You've already had numerous revelations and you will have many more. Enjoy!

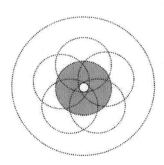

Chapters

These Chapters started off as individual pamphlets. It was a style I had used in my ministry work, consulting/coaching, and college teaching. Once I started weaving the pamphlets into this book form, several Chapters grew, some combined, and brand new ones were co-created.

There is an intended order to the Chapters, but each one also stands on its own. It will become obvious how the basic ideas appear again and again, sometimes in the same recognizable language, but more often in related dialects.

What is a "Swimming Hole"?

You'll see a box or two at the end of each Chapter. Check them out independently if you like. They are intended to be places for ideas to swim around more freely.

My wife asked, *"Is it a 'hole' or more like a lake or ocean?"* I said something like, *"It's not an ocean or lake, but more like a **swimming hole** where you and a few friends might go to have some fun. It's deep enough for diving and probably formed by a creek or very small river; but, of course, it's just an analogy."*

As I look them over, there are no two that suggest a pattern. I marvel at how and when they appeared in the writing process. You may find them fun—and also a bit provocative.

If this metaphor works for you, I encourage you to write your own *Swimming Hole* entries of any length in order to get down on paper the thoughts swimming around in your mind after reading something that stirs your waters.

Part One

You are not what you thought.

> "The problem is that we download our perceptions and beliefs about life years before we acquire the ability for critical thinking. When, as young children, we download limiting or sabotaging beliefs, those perceptions or misperceptions become our *truths*. If our platform is one of misperception, our sub-conscious mind will dutifully generate behaviors that are coherent with those programmed *truths*." (*Spontaneous Evolution*) (my *emphasis*)

There are so many teachings concerning who and what "You" are. My perspective may possibly be a new one for you.

At a meeting where I was asked to introduce my book, I started by passing out the 'Gallery' of individual cards that you see toward the back and then asked for questions from the audience. The discussion that followed lasted well over an hour. Toward the end, a 'senior' participant shared that years ago he had read Norman Vincent Peale's book, *The Power of Positive Thinking* and adopted its perspective: "You" are the sum total of everything that ever happened to you.

From our relatively short discussion, he felt 'my' perspective would work much better for him. He had agreed with a simple, defined way to understand "You" many years ago and was now able to compare and contrast it with the new perspective I was giving. Whether or not you have a clearly defined way to see yourself, I'm optimistic that this new pair of glasses will change your life for the better.

Many teachers follow the *Positive Thinking* model and make "You" a vast collection of things to the point of making you the Universe. Those approaches fall short in helping me understand and deal with the inner and outer conflicts of this world. I look forward to hearing from you one of these days about how this book has worked for you.

A student poster from Personal & Community Health class.

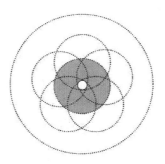

1.

We see the world through our beliefs

We see the world through our beliefs.

Is it time to change your glasses?

Copyright © 2015 Value Life Associates

The Spring of 2016, I played the Magistrate in a Neil Simon play called ***Fools, A Comic Fable***. It's about a town cursed with stupidity for 200 years. How is this possible? Here is the key understanding delivered by the new visiting schoolteacher, Leon, to his new stupid girlfriend, Sophia:

> If a parent tells you you are a naughty child from the day you were born, you will grow up **believing** you are a worthless human being. And from the day you were born, you were told you were all stupid. Now do you understand?

Alas, due to the curse, she is too stupid to understand. They **believed** the curse of stupidity could only be lifted if certain terms were met. When Leon devised a slight-of-hand trick and got them to **believe** the requirements *had* been met, they instantly became smart. A sad but clever comedy revealing how controllable people are.

We (all individual beings/souls)
see (perceive/understand)
the world (both inner and outer)
through our beliefs (*memes*/paradigms/opinions).

Early on, as we see and hear things, our worldview develops without a discernment filter. Ray Dodd, author of ***The Toltec Secret to Happiness***, said,

> Other people's opinions are like seeds. Heard often enough, we begin to believe them. But we begin to see through a filter, a lens of our beliefs and agreements about everything. Every word people say is in some way modified by what they believe – their personal myth. Like all myths, it may not actually be true. Remember, we don't see the world as it is – we see the world as we ~~are~~ [believe].

I had a technical problem with the very last word, so I changed it. Why? Because it is my present **belief** that I am NOT my thoughts. I have thoughts, but they are not me. Since beliefs are thoughts, I am also not my **beliefs**. I understand that I **see** the world through the **beliefs** I have acquired.

Everything we see gets filtered through the lens of our unique, personal set of **beliefs** or paradigms (pairs of glasses). In their book, ***The Spirit and Science of Holistic Health***, Robison and Carrier state,

> Thus, our personal vision of reality is likely to be influenced concurrently by
> *a human paradigm,*
> *a Western civilization paradigm,*
> *an American paradigm,*
> *a community (subculture) paradigm,*
> *an age-specific paradigm, and so on.*

The "so on" could include our color paradigm, our ethnic paradigm, and our club, group, church or political party paradigm. It is not difficult to understand how each of us live in our own personal reality—our own private perception of the world.

We've been cautioned on judging others until we "Walk a mile in their shoes." I believe, as much as we may try, *that* will never happen. Acting the part of another person is always temporary—it lasts until the end of the run. In his 1959 book, ***Black Like Me***, John Howard Griffin, told how Blacks were treated in the South.

He had had his skin medically altered to temporarily be black. He then traveled through several southern states to experience being Black, but he could never *feel* like a Black man in the White man's world. He could and did call a White friend to come pick him up whenever he got tired. Inside his mind, he was still White. It was a useful experience for exposing the severity and depth of the racial divide, but it was acting.

"Why can't everybody just get along?" Perhaps you are seeing why *that* is so hard to do. Do you get along with everybody?

Why not? You may even have a hard time getting along with some of your own conflicting thoughts, feelings and actions. Maybe you can reflect on that.

Even having Merlin as a teacher/mentor did not make everybody get along in Wart's world. Merlin turned him into a fish, a squirrel, and a hawk so he could see the world through their eyes. It did personally help Wart when he became King Arthur, but the rest of the people he dealt with had not had his upbringing.

It may look like the statement and the question on the card are referring to two different worlds. They were meant to be the same world. What will it take to give *you* peace of mind? If you don't find inner peace of mind, you probably won't have authentic peace with the people you encounter. If you judge and condemn others, you'll also notice self-condemning ideas in your own mind.

One of my favorite 'mirrors' for students was playing ***The Weather Robot***. I'd stand up by the chalk board where I had drawn the semblance of a window. With my best robotic movements and speech, I would look 'out' the window and say, "Cloudy day, I'm going to have a dreary, depressing day. I just can't do anything on a cloudy day." I once again looked 'out' the window and said, "Sunny day! What a beautiful, fantastic day. I feel like getting out and doing something today! I love sunny days."

So often we are conditioned to feel a certain way in relation to the weather. We don't even have to wait for the weather. We can start feeling bad on Monday when the TV weather person says,

"We have a big rain in the forecast for Saturday and Sunday. You might as well cancel your plans for a fun weekend; it's going to be a bummer."

A juke box is one of a variety of metaphors for our built-in 'tapes' that intentionally or unintentionally get 'triggered' by the words, actions, or tone of voice of another person. Case in point:

I observed a very common habit at a lecture being given by Dr. Dan Siegel at a **National Wellness Conference**. Someone sneezed and a hundred or more said, "Bless you." Dan said,

> "Okay, everybody, say, 'Bless you,' for all the people who may sneeze in the next hour."

He knew that without clearly giving that instruction, his talk could have been continually interrupted by the mindless habit of many in the room. No one said it after that when several people sneezed.

Where did that habit come from? Do you do it? Is it based on a valid belief or is it simply 'monkey-see-monkey-do'? At Snopes.com I found that saying "Bless you" after sneezing was well researched. Six of the most common **beliefs** about it were listed ending with this:

> So many explanations—each deeply **believed**—for such a simple and often unquestioned practice. And we'll never know which one [if any] is right.

If we see the world through our beliefs, "How do you see the world?" That could refer to your inner world or your outer world. Concerning the outer world; do you **believe** it is 'going to hell in a hand basket' or maybe that 'everything happens for a reason'?

The streets, media, movies, and video games portray one war after another, shooting after shooting, and it is not hard to see how so many people have a negative world view. Many get taught by (false) prophets to fear the future: "The end is near!"

Some of you have a familiarity with the **Bible**.

> "For God has not given us the spirit of fear; but of power, and of love, and of a sound mind." (2Ti.1:7)

1Jo. 5:18 says, "Fear has torment." That doesn't make fear sound very good. In the same verse, it says, "There is no fear in love; but perfect love casts out fear." Hmm. What do you believe? Do you believe the Bible has some good ideas now and then? Maybe you believe it is the word of *God*. Regardless, would you rather live in love or in fear? Fear results from **believing** in some imagined future that has not happened and may never happen. Love also results from a **belief**.

What **belief** produces a loving feeling, attitude, expression, or point of view? Do you love because of genetics? Does love have rules? What is the **belief** you have or need to have to love yourself and/or others? The fear or hate of someone is based on a **belief**. To shift from fear or hate to love requires a paradigm shift—changing your **belief**.

Beliefs are ideas—*memes* we have agreed with whether intentionally or unintentionally. *The Matrix* portrays most people living their lives in a fantasy illusion controlled by *meme-made machinery*. What is reality? For you and me, we each have our own reality. There's much yet to learn about ourselves and this living Universe.

Tools for this mountainous job are sprinkled throughout this and other books. I suggest you climb the mountain one step at a time. **Self-examination** is an important tool. Whenever you notice yourself making a judgment of someone or condemning an idea, make a note to find out what **beliefs** caused you to see things that way. When did you acquire those **beliefs**? Are they important enough to hang on to? Are they good for your health? Are they kind toward others? Are they true? What makes them true or false?

You have already changed many **beliefs** in your life. Think back and make a few notes of things you once believed and now don't. How did you make a change then? Did you realize it wasn't true and just let it go? Did you hear a different point of view and **substitute** the new one for the old? Did you find out that a habit of yours had no basis in fact?

I like to see my beliefs challenged. They don't change easily, but I am a life-long learner and I realize I am ignorant of more things than I know. **Understanding** excites me and *that* comes by making life a quest—a journey of seeking deeper answers to the great mysteries.

Here is an exercise: start a mind map by drawing many circles on a piece of paper around a central circle. Write a core **belief** in the center circle and other **beliefs** in the surrounding circles

Sample of a Mind Map

I was a little surprised at what my circles revealed. I see that there have been several changes this last year in how I see the world. You don't have to write a book about your beliefs and philosophies to see some changes take place in your life, too.

Swimming Hole #1

It's 2016 and the world is swimming in fear and finger-pointing. Each of us sees the world through our unique mixture of beliefs, yet we clump together with others who seem to hold at least one belief that sounds a lot like ours.

Some believe everything is happening according to a pre-written script and there's nothing humans can do to change it. Others believe in "The Realm of Infinite Possibilities."

Some act as the saviors of the world and others passively wait for their savior to appear. Which person is 'right'?

Each of us feels our belief is 'right' with varying degrees of emotion attached. Some act out their beliefs with violence toward others and/or themselves. We read about large numbers of US soldiers committing suicide and about other soldiers being given the label *suicide bombers*.

What is your dream for the world or have you given up on holding a dream? We see the phrases "Be the Dream," "Live the Dream," "Dream Big," "I have a dream," "Life is but a dream," and "Awaken the Dreamer."

Another approach explores "The Possible Human," "The Possible Society," and "The Possible World." Sherlock and others speculate on the likely probabilities based on past performances.

As a career health teacher, I ask, "*What is healthy for me, my community, and the world?*"

I PLEDGE:

MY HEAD TO CLEARER THINKING,

MY HEART TO GREATER LOYALTY,

MY HANDS TO LARGER SERVICE,

MY HEALTH TO BETTER LIVING,

FOR MY CLUB,

MY COMMUNITY,

MY COUNTRY,

AND MY WORLD.

4-H Pledge Poster

2.

Do you do things you don't want to do?

Do YOU ever do things
YOU don't want to do?

YOU   YOU

Which *YOU* is you?

Copyright © 2015 Value Life Associates

Will the Real <u>you</u> Please Stand Up?

Six decades of the game show, *To Tell the Truth*, might tell you where this question comes from. True to form, the above card shows three different 'you's and I will make the case that only one of them is the real <u>you</u>. I am calling the first YOU your body since your body is what actually does things. The second *YOU* represents the thoughts you hear that complain about or praise what your body is doing. The third <u>you</u> will be revealed as the real <u>you</u>.

Seven Questions

(1) **Do you ever do things you don't want to do?** Did you say, "Of course, doesn't everybody?" If you didn't, you probably did for many years of your life. In my last thirty years of college teaching, 100% of my students answered "Yes" to this initial question before there was any explanation offered.

(2) **Why do you do those things?** I would have students call out their answers and I would write them on the chalk board. Please make your own list. Here are a few of the answers from those classes:

Somebody's got to do it.	To get to my goal.	To get paid.
To keep my job.	I've always done it.	Habit.
To be accepted - liked.	I have to.	Tradition.

(3) **Why don't you want to do them?** Again, please make your own list. Here are a few answers others have given over the years.

It's boring.	It's too early in the morning.
I hate it.	It doesn't pay enough..
It's dangerous.	It's not really my job.

(4) **Are you happy doing things you don't want to do?** Happy doesn't seem to fit here. Since you are not happy doing those things, you sometimes find yourself overcompensating doing other things to make you happy. For some it's alcohol and/or other drugs; for others, it's escaping with food, shopping, TV, sleep or taking risks. Some use the creative arts, exercise, meditation, music, spiritual communities and/or books.

(5) **Is it a healthy thing to do?** Your body chemistry produces hormones and neurotransmitters that work against your health when you feel afraid, angry, depressed, helpless or hopeless. If you chronically do things you don't want to do, it works against your body's immune system and sex drive.

(6) **Is it a loving behavior?** It is next to impossible to love your job, the people you work with, your life situation or yourself when you're doing things you don't want to do.

(7) **Which Y*OU* is you?** To find out who <u>you</u> are and to get to that place where <u>you</u> are only doing those things <u>you</u> want to do is crucial to your happiness, your health, your ability to love and your peace of mind. Seriously examining what's presented here has the possibility—no, the probability—of shifting your life dramatically toward those basic human desires. Depending on your commitment, the shift can happen rather quickly.

Let me ask the original question again as you position your hands like the figure on the card: <u>Do YOU</u> (in your right hand) <u>ever do things that *YOU*</u> (in your left hand) <u>don't want to do</u>? Now, which of those two is really <u>you</u>? The one in the right hand, the left hand, both hands, neither? Have I already told you?

Many of us grow up without distinguishing 'me' from my body that carries 'me' around or 'me' from my almost constant stream of thoughts and more occasional feelings. We do know that the people we relate to are not us. We may have experienced the spiritual realm when we were kids, but didn't know what to call it. We are told by society what we are supposed to be.

I announce a coming quiz and start to write on the chalk board:

1. I am_____.
2. Give 2 adjectives and 1 noun that define the answer to #1.
3-7. I have _____, _____, _____, _____, and _____.
8. I do _____ and
9. _____.
10. I follow-through when_____.

I then give the answers I want them to write on the quiz:

1. I am **an individual**.
2. An individual can be defined as
   a unique, indivisible being (person, soul, or entity).
3-7. I have **a body, thoughts, feelings, relationships, and spirit**.
8. I do **observe when I'm awake (aware)** and
9. **make decisions when given a choice**.
10. I follow-through when I **exercise my power of will**.

Bonus: I am connected **energetically to all that exists**.

I am an Individual:
*a unique, indivisible being (person, soul, entity)
connected energetically to all that exists.*
I have a body, thoughts,
feelings, relationships, and spirit.
I do observe when I'm *awake* (aware)
and make decisions when given a choice.
I follow through when
I exercise my power of will.

We all have unique bodies and minds, but our bodies and minds are divisible. Indivisible means "cannot be divided." Our bodies get divided all the time. We clip or bite our nails; all the cells in our bodies get replaced every seven years (some get replaced every day); and we lose body parts to accidents or surgery. This means that you, the individual, have a body, but you are not your body. Why? Because you are indivisible (you cannot be divided from you). That also means that you, the soul, are genderless. Gender is a genetic, hormonal, body thing; at least until awareness and beliefs mix in.

The same goes for the mind or intellect. Each person's mind is unique, but we all experience a division within our minds when we recognize opposing ideas. "I have to do this, **but** I don't want to do it." All those complaining thoughts you observe when your body is doing those things *YOU* don't want to do is evidence of a divided mind. I'll slip in a Bible verse that states this very point:

A double minded man is unstable in all his ways. (Jam.1:8)

When you change your mind, you're still the same you. I have a mind (thoughts), but I am not my mind.

Feelings get divided. Desire competes with fear. Pain competes with comfort. Hope competes with hopelessness.

We all have relationships and we've all experienced the loss of a friend, a family member, a pet, a home or familiar space, a plant in our care, and various possessions. The loss can be caused by a death, downsizing or many other reasons. As much as we feel energetically connected to *that* being or thing, we know that *it* is not us.

Some say we all have spirit, even though it is harder to define or nail down. For this section, I use spirit to refer to things like holy versus evil, meaning to life versus meaningless existence, enthusiasm versus slothfulness, and assurance versus doubt. Just seeing this list makes it clear that spirit can be divided; therefore, I am not my spirit.

Throughout the book, you will see **I** am described equally as…

a unique, indivisible being, person, soul, or entity.
a gardener.
a pod of consciousness.
an observer.
a decision-maker.
the Self.
an individual.

You will also see this symbol:

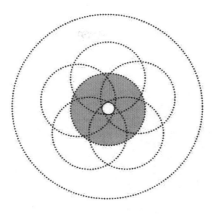

I constructed this Big Picture symbol representing the individual **Self** (central white circle) in the midst of its seven dimensions: the personal physical, intellectual, and emotional; the social, spiritual (shaded central circle), and vocational; and the environmental (large outer circle).

As you, the individual, expand your awareness of these dimensions and move toward the fulfillment of your potentials, you make wiser, more informed decisions when you're presented with choices.

Your environment goes from the micro to the macro. Your personal physical space is mid-way between the smallest known micro (Neutrino = 10^{-24}) and the largest known macro (the Universe = 10^{26}). You are **a giant** to one half and a microbe to the other half. [See: scaleofuniverse.com]

Equally amazing, you are energetically connected to all of it. Everything exists in an interconnected energy field that physicists and others are learning more about every day.

We, the individual observers and occasional decision-makers, are privy only to an iota of the whole; and with telescopes and microscopes, we can observe a bit more of the smallest and largest parts of the whole.

You may *feel* insignificant, but you are a contributing part of the whole, as everything else is. Your unique contribution has far-reaching consequences beyond your sensory connections.

Swimming Hole #2

"I am NOT my thoughts" could have more context and texture, so let's do some *swimming around* with that phrase.

I would not know *I* existed without thoughts. *I* would not have thoughts that *I* recognized without my knowledge of words and the meanings they have for me. *I* would not have words without the many relationships that provided me a language within a cultural context.

There could be no relationships without the regenerating and renewing processes of life and reproduction. There is no regeneration without the diverse, sustaining environments of air, food and water. None of these essentials could exist without spirit/energy and the amazing evolution from the element Hydrogen, the most abundant element that we know of, to the living Universe of today.

We're told there would be no Universes if there was not a *"God"* or a *"Big Bang."* We know so much and yet so little.

Does that mean *I* am dependent upon and connected to all of these steps? I say, "Yes." *I* am one of the latest 'pods of consciousness' on the planet. Did *I* exist before or did *I* just appear that day *I* became Self-aware? Some say *I* arrived on the planet from some 'place' else. I, personally, am not aware of that happening. Others state they know it to be true for themselves. Who am I to argue with someone else's experience or interpretation of experience?

I know; more questions than answers.

3.

You are the Gardener

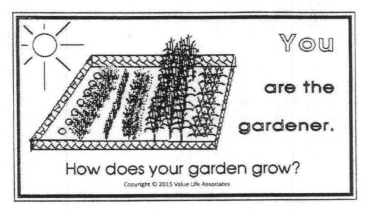

YOU

are the

gardener.

How does your garden grow?

Copyright © 2015 Value Life Associates

At face value, we know the gardener is not the corn, carrots, cabbage or beans; but as a **parable** of our lives, you may find it harder to separate the gardener from the garden. You and things you have (e.g. a body, thoughts, job, relationships, children, beliefs) often blend together. Take a moment and see if the things you have are what *define* you.

I am promoting the belief that **you are the gardener** and **not** the garden. I believe you are an individual (entity, being, soul) that observes your garden (body, thoughts, feelings, relationships, environment and spirit) and makes the best decisions possible whenever you're aware of having a choice. Your awareness can greatly expand and deepen and this will allow you to make even better, wiser decisions. I believe you **can** have limited—but important—control over your internal and external environments.

Is your garden neat and tidy like the card pictures? When did you last take inventory? Do you really know what all is growing there? And, "**When, exactly, did you become the gardener?**"

I believe you're no different than me in growing up with several, even hundreds of people, acting as your gardener. Each poked their share of seeds into your fertile mind. For the most part, you did not ask for their input and had few real defenses to stop them. Each of those surrogate gardeners had their own point of view based on the unique set of beliefs growing in their gardens.

27

These diverse plantings self-organize in ways that motivate us, trouble us, confuse us, and define who we think we are and why we're here. I share a few examples I have encountered through my life. What is your 'sunflower' that you don't mind people seeing?

Discordant Beliefs: Science and *God* Meet

Today, whatever age you are, is the right time to be examining your own garden in greater and greater detail. Those **discordant beliefs** of competing gardeners contributed to the emerging set of values you now live by. They are political, family, religious, and economic (to name a few).

A powerful example of this **discord** came up in my **Psychology of Sport** class one day. Students challenged a point I was making from scientific research. It led to a discussion comparing science and religion. It was ironic that their careers would depend on scientific understanding, but they doubted *all* science because they believed it contradicted their Christian beliefs. Their belief in *God* and creation versus Darwin and evolution was *that* powerful; it brought *all* science into question.

They were surprised to learn the sequence in which life-forms were created in Genesis 1. When they saw that Day 3 and Day 5 should really be reversed they became more curious. Then, when the students also saw that *they* were only concerned with *who* did the creating in contrast to scientists who were only concerned with *how* it all happened, I could feel a slight shift in their thinking. I believe Genesis 1 and evolution *can* co-exist.

CREATION	EVOLUTION
Based on the Bible	Based on Science
Asks, "**Who** did it?"	Asks, "**How** did it happen?"
Answer: *God*	Answers: **still pouring in**

The sequence of life forms created (Genesis 1)

3rd Day: Dry land brings forth plants
5th Day: The fish, fowl, and moving creatures with life
6th Day: Beasts of the field
6th Day (later): male and female humans

Does Science agree with this sequence? Do you?

A "day" refers to "the process of time"
(How could there be land plants before the 4th day?)

I commonly presented the above chart each semester in my **Personal and Community Health** classes. It reveals a needless debate over *apples* and *oranges*. Science and religion are generally asking different questions. Creationist are satisfied with the answer to "*Who* done it?" found in Genesis 1: *God*—end of inquiry. Evolutionists have not found all the answers to their many "*How*" questions and are continuing to search for missing pieces of the puzzle.

I would finish this discussion with a posting of Romans 1:20 (KJV) on the overhead:

> For the invisible things of him from the creation of the world are clearly seen, being understood by the things that are made, even his eternal power and Godhead; so that they are without excuse:

When you check out the context, you'll find "the invisible things of him" refers to the things of *God*. This is so interesting to me. Paul says the invisible things of *God*, including *God's* eternal power and *Godhead*, **are clearly seen, being understood by the things that are made.** Can *God* and *God's* power be understood?

29

I've heard many church people say, "No." But Paul says, Yes!

Who is looking at **the things that are made**? Church leaders or scientists? The essence of a scientist is to **understand the things that are made**. Some say scientists may even understand the invisible things of *God* before the church leaders do.

You may be wondering how the Bible can be used in a public university class. As you saw in this case, students were blocked from accepting scientific understandings taught in their academic classes because of their indoctrinated religious views.

These students volunteered that they were Christians. Having a working knowledge of the Bible, I was able to offer them a perspective that allowed for **both** their personal religious beliefs **and** the findings of science. I had no intention of challenging their biblical beliefs; only in looking at them with a broader perspective. I also taught the **new biology of** epigenetics that is partially replacing Darwin's dominance in biology. [See YouTube: Epigenetics-Tyson]

War: Fighting it outwardly and/or inwardly

> War will exist until that distant day
> when the conscientious objector
> enjoys the same reputation and prestige
> that the warrior does today.
>   John F. Kennedy

Conscientious objectors have stood out in human history. They have been the game changers. Some look to Jesus as their standard of objecting to the status quo due to conscience; but everywhere you look, you'll see it; you'll see it whenever people stand up and object to the inhumane treatment of other people, of animals, of the earth, water and air.

Indoctrination often **blinds** us to alternative viewpoints. Some soldiers ordered to Vietnam, Iraq or Afghanistan felt a deep conflict of values. *Do to others as you'd have them do to you* or kill and risk your own life for sometimes questionable or conflicting causes? For many, the fighting continues inside when they come home. This is explained by a story commonly told about the Dalai Lama:

"Why didn't you fight back against the Chinese?"

The Dalai Lama looked down, swung his feet just a bit,
then looked back up at us and said with a gentle smile,

"Well, war is obsolete, you know."

Then, after a few moments, his face grave, he said,

"Of course, the mind can rationalize fighting back...
but the heart, the heart would never understand.
Then you would be divided in yourself...
the heart and the mind...and <u>the war would be inside you</u>."

Moral injury is a well-documented label in clinical psychology. The following quote from a government website clearly defines it:

> Like psychological trauma, moral injury is a construct that describes extreme and unprecedented life experience including the harmful aftermath of exposure to such events. Events are considered morally injurious if they "transgress deeply held moral beliefs and expectations" (1). Thus, the key precondition for moral injury is an act of transgression, which shatters moral and ethical expectations that are rooted in religious or spiritual beliefs, or culture-based, organizational, and group-based rules about fairness, the value of life, and so forth.

Moral injury in war

> In the context of war, moral injuries may stem from direct participation in acts of combat, such as killing or harming others, or indirect acts, such as witnessing death or dying, failing to prevent immoral acts of others, or giving or receiving orders that are perceived as gross moral violations (2). The act may have been carried out by an individual or a group, through a decision made individually or as a response to orders given by leaders.
> http://www.ptsd.va.gov/professional/co-occurring/moral_injury_at_war.asp

More than 1.7 million young adults got draft notices during the Vietnam War years, including me. Each one could tell you a story. World heavyweight boxing champ Muhammad Ali was one who followed his conscience on April 28, 1967, and refused to be drafted into the Army. He did not let patriotic propaganda blind his conscience.

> *Why should they ask me to put on a uniform and go ten thousand miles from home and drop bombs and bullets on brown people in Vietnam while so-called Negro people in Louisville are treated like dogs and denied simple human rights?*
>
> *...I have nothing to lose by standing up for my beliefs. So I'll go to jail.*
>
> *We've been in jail for four hundred years.*
>
> Muhammad Ali

Years earlier, Dr. Martin Luther King, Jr was 'drafted' to help lead the Civil Rights Movement. Up until April 1967, his focus was almost exclusively on Civil Rights; but through much prayer and reflection, his worldview broadened and he began speaking out against the Vietnam war, institutional racism and the plague of poverty wherever it occurred in the world. He called them ***the triple threat to human rights*** (Militarism, Racism and Materialism).

Because of his broadened statement of conscience, most of his friends, colleagues and President Johnson turned against him. One year later, he was murdered. But he had "*been to the mountain*" and was not afraid to give his life for what he believed was the right thing to do. Those that had him killed died conflicted and depressed.

What did I do? I refused my orders to Vietnam in January of 1968 by going AWOL and turning myself in 31 days later. Why? When I was a kid, I got a BB gun for Christmas. Playing around I hit a bird in the back yard. It fell to the ground flapping its wings. I ran to it in a panic. With a large rock, I ended its suffering and made the rock its tombstone, complete with a cross. I had just experienced a Moral Injury. I vowed never to pick up a gun again.

Fast-forward to 1966. I had just graduated college and was headed to Yale Divinity School for the fall semester. At a **National Student YMCA** conference in Chicago where I was just elected a national vice-president, someone ran up and said my dad was on the phone. Dad said I had received my draft notice and better come home.

I knew I wasn't going to carry a gun so I enlisted in the Navy and went to **Hospital Corpsman School**. I would help the sick and injured. About that time, the Pentagon changed a policy and started requiring Navy Corpsmen serving as medics for the Marines to carry and use rifles as a regular Marine. I knew I wasn't going to carry a gun so I sought counsel from officers, chaplains, and finally the **War Resisters League** (WRL).

Navy admin said I <u>had</u> to go to Vietnam as a Marine medic. The **WRL** said the military game forced me to go AWOL for 30 days, turn myself in, get Court Martialed, and if I lost, do it all over again. I had to go AWOL twice and serve five months in the brig. From there I received an honorable discharge.

Life's Plantings: Body Parts and More

I've decided **not** to skim over an area that gets labeled *too dark* or *TMI*. Your *parent* may want you to skip this, but it may serve as a tool to help you dig deeper in your own garden for the purpose of understanding some more of your inner battles.

Even though I know the names of many of my school teachers, I cannot tell you much about *what* they planted in my garden. The following indelible images, flavored with feelings, were planted by the most unlikely *teachers*. In the church these images were all labeled *evil spirits* that needed to be cast out. That did not work well.

Post-church teachings of the secular world helped me honor these images and their messengers as part of the stream of life that has brought me to this moment. They are no longer *evil*.

My parents were very discreet. I only saw my dad's backside once and my mother's breasts once (I was 16). I had one brother three years older and two brothers six and seven years younger. I don't remember it, but I was told a neighbor girl and I took baths together when we were three or four.

At school, three of us boys watched from a classroom window as a younger boy led a young girl behind the bushy fence of the playground. As the two boys watched, one used the phrase "stinky finger." We were in the first grade. By the fourth grade, that younger boy was pimping the girl to a few boys for a peek or a touch. The *angel* and *devil* argued; I said, "No."

Another schoolmate invited me to his house only one time. On that occasion, he pulled out a shoebox of photos saying his father had brought them back from the war. The only one I remember was of a woman squatting with her legs open and her genitals exposed. I felt bad for her.

I was a Safety Patrolman in the 4th grade. At my post one day, a man wearing a trench coat came right up to me and showed me one of those series of three pictures you get in the booth at the bus station. They showed the head of a woman and the trunk of a man as she performed oral sex on him.

I was asked to babysit the younger daughter of friends of my parents. They knew they could trust me to be *good*. I was shocked when she came into the TV room and stood on the couch as she watched the TV, completely disrobed, and put on her full-body pajamas with feet.

My older brother and his neighborhood gang seldom included me in their activities. Here is one time they did:

> They came into my basement bedroom wanting to include me in a card game they called "Strip Poker." As a 1st grader, I was excited to be included and even more excited when "I won" (meaning to them that I lost **my** clothes first). They tried to think up things to do with me and for me to do and it was all very exciting.

My older brother 'inherited' a box of **Playboy** magazines from a tenant and kept them in his *private* bedroom. I was ten when I snuck in one day and got an eye-full.

In the sixth grade, I was with several female classmates touring a friend's empty house before it was sold. In one room, on a ladder step, was a nudist magazine. The girls picked it up and started looking. They showed me this page of a naked girl leaning up against a tree. I wanted to take the magazine home, but I was too embarrassed to even continue to look at it.

On the 6th grade class picnic to Devil's Backbone, I left the group as they ate under the big tree and walked up the hillside covered with very tall grass turned brown. I could look down and see them, but they could not see me. For the first time in my life, I stripped naked and laid down in the grass. I felt happy.

My father managed and then owned a women's clothing store in town. I worked there off and on my whole growing up years. It had a dozen or so mannequins, half in the windows and half stored in the basement. I thought they were *pretty special*; I could touch them. There were also dressing rooms and I did my best to catch a peek whenever I could get away with it.

Somewhere in those elementary years, I noticed a book on our bookshelf in the back bedroom. It was the illustrated version of Dante's **Divine Comedy**. It had many pen-and-ink drawings by

Gustave Dore of naked men and women in various stages of torture. Here is one.

Very few of those events were planned. They all contributed to the lenses I looked through to view myself and the world. I felt a void in my life. I *longed* for intimacy, closeness, and affection. My household did not provide it and no one in my community provided it. I could only fantasize fulfillment. Each of you has your own unique series of stories.

We all grew up using (or being used by) **defense mechanisms** to protect us from the hurtful situations we encountered. [See Chapter 11] One of mine was to be the *good boy* in seeking affection from my mother. This required me to hide anything I thought Mom might consider *bad*. That meant I could not tell my brothers, or anyone else, my secret pains, pleasures or fantasies. I also repressed my angers, lied, and feared rejection. Something shifted when Mom forgot to show up at my third-grade Mother's Day party. Each of us had made significant preparations. She was the only mother missing. I was devastated.

Health experts agree that shedding these defenses allows us to mature in a healthy manner, but far too many of us continue them right on through our teen and adult lives with varying unintended health consequences. Mine was prostate cancer.

At church, my childhood fear to confess certain things did not help me reconcile my childhood experiences or continued *longing*. My new marriage began to help, but my over-responsible dedication to ministry work (I was a *really* good boy) short-circuited progress. At one point, I just wanted to be a *eunuch*; by the time we left the church in 2000, in essence, I was.

These *secret* stories reveal only one of the themes of my life. I didn't know it then, but the images and events were NOT me! I observed them, wrestled with them, and wondered about them. I knew I wanted to be happy and, like everyone else, was happy from time to time. I now honor them as steps in the larger story that co-created my future.

You have your own *secrets* and maybe you have had the ability to trust another soul with yours. At the least, write them out and see if you can understand that *everyone* involved was, for the most part, acting out the habits started in their youth. It does not help to condemn them. In fact, condemning them exposes your own judging *virus*. [See Chapter 6]

Many societies fear or condemn nudity while private pornography and naturalism have become the outlets of naked expression throughout the world. Individuals in the LGBT community have been threatened, condemned, and killed due to bigoted indoctrination and ignorance. Ideas in the Bible have fueled much of the bigotry. Few people understand the broad range of genetic hormonal expression humanity has always had and will continue to co-create.

I sometimes played the role of a hypocrite minister during my twenty-five years, teaching some things I did not believe and doing some things we taught were *evil*. My wife and I moved on. I have done my best to stop playing the hypocrite role.

Since leaving the church, I have nurtured a kindness and gentleness toward myself that I had not experienced during those church years. I am grateful for **all** my past. I condemn no one. I'm sure my actions hurt several people back there and I have learned to forgive myself for those actions. I did the best I could do.

Max Ehrmann's beautiful ***Desiderata*** (1952) includes the phrase that sums up much of this for me:

> **"...be gentle with yourself."**

By Design: Our *Meme*-made Materialism

There are other areas where people can and do make moral choices. In 1980, there were very few designers and architects who had the vision and the willingness to design products free of the toxins and pollutants that injure and/or kill the future for many. The ones that **questioned the continued use** of these toxins met stiff resistance from the industry. What to do?

In 2002, chemist Michael Braungart and architect William McDonough published their book, *Cradle to Cradle*. As a new manufacturing standard, they encouraged all product designers everywhere to plan with this intention:

> ## Love all the children
> ## of all species
> ## for all time.

During the 1990s, they had done their homework and found resources, materials, and companies willing to make their products without the use of any ingredients that would harm anybody or anything in any way. They demonstrated that it was possible to make the products and tools of living without toxins and pollutants. Some manufacturers are now doing it. It takes that core **belief** which more and more people see is not just a pipe dream, but a necessity if civilization is to survive.

Why do we let *memes* drive us to design and make products that are toxic to all the children of all species for all time? Is it just robot behavior? Is the system so big and powerful that "resistance is futile"? I believe the polluters are stuck in an old paradigm. They will not be pushed into changing their beliefs, but the clean alternative can be made so attractive and profitable that they will be curious enough to learn more.

I have shared a few examples of old world-views and new world-views. It is difficult to change our glasses/paradigms and see the world differently, but we have all seen how education and travel (physically and virtually) have already helped *us* do it. I see that you are still open to exploring other perspectives? May we find our role in **loving all the children of all species for all time.**

We are at another turning point in human history when the examination of our beliefs and values can contribute to a seismic shift that is making global values more humane. We get to become the true gardeners of our **beliefs**. It is hard work, but indoctrinated *status quo* **beliefs** don't work well in this dynamically changing world.

Swimming Hole #3

Patriotism stirs many emotions. It both unifies and separates. Patriotism is an idea. I confess I have a problem with this meme.

I just finished reading a book I saw in my home in the late forties, *Three Came Home* by Agnes Newton Keith. She, with her husband and young son, barely survived the Japanese prison camps of North Borneo. The book details their experiences.

Bullied on a US transport ship home she reflected: "When the Japanese browbeat, bullied, and humiliated us I had been able to comfort myself by saying, 'But Americans don't do that!'

"Meanwhile, sitting in the lounge talking, listening to the radio broadcasts, we learned the pay-off. The world had not changed ... Love of country flourished, while love of humanity withered; worship of *God* was present, and following of Christ was absent. This was the victory we had won. This was the world men had bought with their blood. This was peace.

"Today we live in a world, not a state. Discoveries of science eliminate space and time.   We have become a body of human beings, not of nationals. The responsibility of the entire body is ours."

In your patriotism, you may love your flag and your country. I just ask you to reflect today, and every day, on this idea: *A body works together to promote the health of the whole; otherwise, the whole body dies. Each of us must do our part to heal this body of human beings. It's the only body we have.*

My Letter to the Editor, News Tribune, June 1, 2016

4.

Who is Driving your Car?

Who is driving your car?

*Where are **they** taking you?*

Copyright © 2015 Value Life Associates

My wife and I were driving up the park road of an extinct volcano in New Mexico the summer of 2013. There was no outside guardrail and the road went up and around counter-clockwise. A little way up I started to feel a force trying to get me to pull the car to the right and plunge to our deaths. I felt as though I was wrestling for control of the steering wheel as the force was trying to use my own muscles against me. When we got to the half-way point parking lot, I parked—visibly shaken—and said, "I'll never drive on a road like that again."

At the time, I did not have a logical or illogical explanation for my wrestling match and, even though the story seems to go along with the card questions, the card was created long before that trip as an **analogy** or **parable**. I think I can do a better job of explaining the analogy than I can that real, visceral experience in New Mexico.

On the surface, this would be a short pamphlet: "I'm driving my car and I go wherever I want to go." Actually, that's the answer most of my students have given over the years; at least until I asked a few more questions. One day in class I put a chair up on the big lab table in front of the room. I climbed up and sat in the chair facing the chalk board wearing an available cap and occasionally sunglasses.

"Who has an imaginary car they haven't been able to afford that I can chauffeur for them?" With some cajoling, I'd get one or two very tentative hands. "What kind of car?" One says, "**A Lexus.**" "Okay, where would you like for me to drive you?" "**Memphis.**" "No, we're not going to Memphis; I want to go see my sick Aunt over in Topeka. You don't mind, do you?" "**No, that's okay, I guess.**"

I call on another student; similar results. In some classes it took four or five students before one said to me, "**You're fired.**" That's when I say, "Thank you. Now I can get down."

The whole point is to <u>fire a chauffeur</u> if they are not driving you where you want them to go. So, you see the analogy. What does the car represent? What gets you around and sort of acts like a car? Yes, your body. Your body goes through the motions of doing things out of habit or obligation, even when you *think* you don't want to.

Do you agree that <u>you</u> are an individual—a unique, indivisible entity or soul? You have a body, but you are not your body. You have ideas or *memes* that 'tell' you what to do. They can be *memes* from people around you or *memes* already conceived in your mind that pop into your conscious awareness. It is not uncommon to hear conflicting instructions or responses to instructions that require you to make a choice. "I can." "**I can't.**" "I should." "**I shouldn't.**" "I want to, **but I'm afraid.**"

Your job is to decide which *meme* (idea or **belief**) will get to drive your car. So, "Who is driving your car?" Yes, I am suggesting that a **belief**, yours or someone else's, is always chauffeuring your car (body). A **belief** can be called a *meme*, a paradigm, an opinion or a world view.

Most of the time, our actions and reactions are *driven* by what Ellen Langer in her book, *Mindfulness*, calls **Pre-Cognitive Commitments** at a subconscious level. Yes, we often behave automatically. Your first mission, if you accept it, is expressed throughout her book and this book in a variety of ways: examine your many **Pre-Cognitive Commitments** that get you to act and react automatically (like a robot). The goal is to carefully observe and listen before you pick a wise response from the menu. None of us want to be a robot, easily controlled by past teachings (*memes*) that we've never taken the time to question or examine.

Here is another classroom example. For years, I would prepare the class for a True/False 'quiz.' "I'm going to make a statement and then I'll ask you to raise your hand if you think it is true or false when I call out 'True' and then 'False.' Are you ready?"

I glare into their eyes with a knowing look and say, **"You are your own worst enemy!** How many say True?" Most of the hundred students raise their hands. "How many say the statement is False?" The most I've had are three out of a hundred.

"The 'correct' answer is False." And the arguments begin. They do their best to defend their **belief** that they, indeed, *are* their own worst enemy. Is that a **belief** you feel you need to defend? **It is a self-condemning belief, isn't it?** Who taught you this idea? Parents? Teachers? Coaches? Ministers? Because the students think it is true and have re-enforced this 'truth' many times by making poor choices, being their own worst enemy becomes an identity, a way of life, their character.

I begin to lay out my case. "Let's look up the word **enemy**."

"Enemy—a person who is actively opposed or hostile to someone or something.

Synonyms: opponent, adversary, foe, archenemy, rival, antagonist, combatant, challenger, competitor, oppose."

It takes *another* person for you to be or have an enemy. Why would someone tell you that **you** are your own worst enemy? Possibly, they had given you some instructions and expected you to perform perfectly right away and when you didn't, they blamed you for it by saying, **"You** are your own worst enemy; I told you not to do that and you turned right around and did it."

For most people, the statement was said so long ago and so often that they can't recall exactly who first told them or when they started believing it. Guilt, self-blame, depression, shame, hopelessness, regret, fear, all have their connections to this powerful phrase that can only be labeled a lie.

When I've asked them the first day of class to write down, "Who or what is your worst enemy?" less than a fourth say, "**I am.**" Why, when I spoke the verbal true/false statement, did 99%

automatically say "**True**"? I believe I manipulated them with my tone of voice and gaze, "**You are your own worst enemy!**" stating it like they heard it said many times by their parents, teachers, coaches and others. However firmly they believe the phrase, it cannot be true.

For the 1971 Earth Day celebration, Pogo stated to Porcupine, "Yep, Son, we have met the enemy and he is us." It was true. As a society, **we were enemies of the Earth**. It takes at least two parties for one to be the enemy of the other; therefore, on a personal level, you **cannot** be your own enemy. You are an <u>indivisible</u> being. You cannot fight yourself. I 'hear' some of you starting to argue with this like several of my students did.

"I have seen the Enemy and it is not US! You are NOT your own worst enemy!"

Copyright © 2015 Value Life Associates

"I know I shouldn't have done that. I'm so stupid. **I am my own worst enemy!**" Can you hear that *other voice* getting involved? It says, "**I**", but it started as a ***bully meme***, spoken by someone in authority, condemning you, their student. Now the ***bully meme*** is inside your own head. These <u>condemning **words** are the enemies of the Soul</u>. They stung at the time and can echo for years, condemning us and feeding our sense of hopelessness. ***Bully memes*** have no compassion, no understanding.

When those judging, condemning ***memes*** are in someone's *driver's seat*, their host is powerless to see things any other way. Old ***memes*** take control of their words, their tone of voice, and their body language. Mercy, mercy. They also must have been bullied.

There are also intuitions that *drive* us. Some attribute these powerful leadings to *God* or similar higher powers. I think you are all familiar with these 'leadings' both on the inspirational side and the warning side. Inspirations include 'getting' a poem, song, tune, vision, revelation or insight from your muse or higher power.

On the warning side, 'something' stops you, whether or not you are conscious of any voice directing you. You may even question, "Why can't I seem to do this?" These *hunches* or *forces*, that have warned us in such powerful ways, compel us to stop what we started to do. We sometimes override their warning and experience some negative consequences. Those of us that have learned to honor the warnings have undoubtedly been spared many a calamity.

Many people report a realm, an energy field, a spirit felt, a word revealed, and sometimes images seen. I had the honor to hear from my mother's mother her account of being visited by her husband who had passed. He stood at the end of her bed looking peaceful and told her he was fine and not to worry. He comforted her with a *knowing* beyond belief.

A trusted colleague and I were talking about this kind of stuff one day when he shared *this* story:

> Some friends and I were at a little town south of here checking out what is referred to as a haunted house. As usual, I was taking pictures outside and inside the house—nobody lived there at that time. It was an uneventful day.
>
> When I got home and developed my film—I do it the old-fashioned way—I was startled. A picture taken of the front porch showed an older woman sitting there in a wheelchair. She was not there when I took the picture. Another picture taken from inside the kitchen looking toward a window showed a young girl in the window.
>
> I showed them to my friends—who were equally shocked—and they decided to do some research. Over a hundred years ago, a woman and a young girl did live there and the woman was in a wheelchair on the second floor. The girl took care of her needs.
>
> My friends then decided to try and contact these 'ghosts' by going there at night, setting up some portable lights that can be turned on with a tap. They set them up on tables around the kitchen. I was there.
>
> One friend led the inquiry. She asked if they, the 'ghosts', were present and told them to tap the light. The light came on. She had a series of questions and they answered them with the tap of a light. I can't explain it, but these 'ghosts' were there.

Sam Schnieder's photo: An EMP peers in the window?

I believe people are getting messages from 'beyond' their understanding every day, all over the world. We can't be certain exactly *where* they come from, but they keep coming. Crop Circles fall into this category when they are not man-made.

One of our precious cats stayed out all night and couldn't be easily found the next morning. I decided to meditate for an image that could lead me to where he was. All I *saw* was a red object and a tall green object behind it. I started walking around the streets of our little neighborhood.

Before I became fully aware of this red car, I noticed on the pavement next to its driver's door, three shiny pennies in a perfectly straight line pointing toward the right front side of the car. When I looked that direction beyond the car, there was a tall evergreen tree encircled with long bows touching the ground. I approached the tree, separated some of the low bows, and there he was, crouching by the trunk. How did all that work?

Many mysteries of life are yet to be revealed; so, learn to choose your *chauffeurs* wisely. Some are qualified to *drive* for the health of the whole planet. Finding qualified *drivers* takes some looking, lots of interviews, and possibly many test-drives. "Happy trails to you, until we meet again."

Swimming Hole #4a

ME (Moving Energy)
Words and tune by R.B. (Dick) Dalton (2015)

When you look at me, what you think you see,
is only Moving Energy.
ME has no start, ME has no end.
In hide and seek ME always wins.
From inside ME I look around
through new and old beliefs I've found.
ME has no start, ME has no end. Is ME real or is ME pretend?

When I'm out at night and I see the stars,
I no longer wonder what they are.
They have no start, they have no end;
they're moving Spirit, like the Wind.
From inside ME I look around
through new and old beliefs I've found.
The Universe, the Love I feel; All is Moving Energy, so real.

When I look at you, what I think I see,
is just another form of ME.
ME has no start, ME has no end;
when you've got ME, you have a friend.
From inside ME I look around
through new and old beliefs I've found.
ME has no start, ME has no end;
when you've got ME, you have a friend.

45

Swimming Hole #4b

And what about that event in New Mexico? Just as we each have personal, positive and negative *Energetic Memory Patterns* (EMPs) that 'drive' our habits, we also live in a universal energy field that contains positive and negative EMPs of others, past and present.

Everything boils down to energy sooner or later. We are told we have energy fields that extend a good way beyond our skin. Sitting next to someone, our energetic fields are mingling. Some people exude more positive energy, others more negative. The field of **Energy Medicine** is getting results.

We read of so much research on the energies of atoms, crystals, plants, people, prayer, meditation, and intentions; entanglement, entrainment, inspiration; mediums, healers, shamans; past-lives, near-death experiences, Indigo children; orbs, ghosts, visions, voices; and the list goes on.

Maybe you have visited a *sacred* space where you physically felt a holy EMP. There are also *haunted* spaces where EMPs are 'stuck.' When we encounter such a space, as I did in New Mexico, and have receptors tuned to the right frequency, the EMP can 'take hold.'

I was told by one researcher in this area that 'dead' people whose EMP is 'stuck' can be released by acknowledging the 'person.' I could not see the 'person' I was wrestling, but I have since taken quiet time to both acknowledge and forgive them.

So many people have experienced these paranormal events that they are almost to the point of normal. I suggest we not criticize those who report their energetic experiences. What do *we* know? Certainly, we know we all have a lot more to learn.

I Am NOT My Thoughts!

Part Two

Let's stop playing the deadly game of blaming

SPONTANEOUS EVOLUTION: OUR POSITIVE FUTURE (AND A WAY TO GET THERE FROM HERE) by Bruce H. Lipton and Steve Bhaerman put so many things in perspective for me that I used it as a textbook in one of my Wellness major classes. This quote will sound as though you have read it twenty times already in this book. I share it to show the universality of this understanding.

> "We have been shackled with emotional chains wrought by dysfunctional behaviors, programmed by the stories of the past. Through forgiveness, we unshackle ourselves and others, allowing all of us to let go of the old story. Then, and only then, will we be free to create our positive future."
> *Spontaneous Evolution p.42*

During those early years (1-6), we are misjudged by those around us. The practice of misjudging (blaming and condemning) becomes part of our daily behavior when we do not understand the true causes of anyone's behaviors. This practice will continue throughout life unless we have a revelation that convinces us to look at ourselves and others with more understanding and compassion.

The next student poster describes the universal process. The word "excellence" could be replaced with "judging" or many other terms. Until these habits of mind and body are examined closely and without favor, they continue.

Part Two shows more of the cultivation and consequences of the deadly blame game. You will see more exercises and new ways of looking at things that can help you substitute new, life-promoting habits for the old, destructive ones.

Student poster from a Health class years ago.

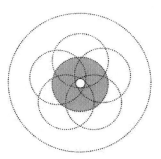

5.

Suicide victims: Murdered???

We have seen wave after wave of suicide hit our community and nation. Some of us have lost friends. We will miss them, more than they will ever know. We can't bring them back; we can't change the past; but we can learn to understand what brings about a decision to stop living.

We are all struggling to live; struggle isn't limited to a few special people. Many of us may not realize what the real struggle is over, much less where it takes place. We are **not** our own worst enemy, as some try to teach; but powerful forces have invaded us and can become an engine pulling a train of thoughts and feelings that sometimes lead to deadly consequences.

These forces are mental pathogens that sicken our minds and bodies. **Just like a virus** invades the body and spreads by killing as many cells as it can; **cruel words, attitudes, and images invade our minds.** They infect our self-image and memories; steal our happiness, our hope, our trust, and peace of mind; and, yes, even take our life.

We all know rejection, hurt, fear, guilt, confusion, doubt, hate, hopelessness, anger, and resentment; and we remember some of the memories they are attached to. We were not born with those thoughts and feelings already in us. They invaded us just like a virus.

We had very little power to resist them, and the more they hit us, the weaker our resistance got; the more we thought on them, the stronger they grew. We felt helpless and soon identified with some of the images they formed.

They came into our minds as we were growing up. They told us we were stupid or ugly or not worth someone's time or that we were "*a pain in the butt*" to somebody. They hollered at us and said cruel things to us that hurt us very deeply. "*You can't do anything right.*" "*I don't like you anymore.*" "*You'll never amount to anything.*"

People were the vehicles that passed these attitudes and thoughts on to us **just like a virus gets spread**. Some of us grew to hate those people and blame those people that said those cruel things, when all the time, the people were just doing to us what others had done to them, not having the knowledge or the power to stop the contagion.

If we weren't given enough love, positive words, or attitudes to fight back against those negative thoughts and feelings; they easily overtook us. Many of us became slaves to those depressing ideas. "*I'm stupid.*" "*I'm ugly.*" "*I'm my own worst enemy.*" "*I'm bad.*" "*Nobody likes me.*" "*I can't do anything right.*" "*Why try? I'll never amount to anything.*" Some of us felt the pressure to do more and more to try and please others. A few of us found temporary relief from the pain by using various drugs. We knew we didn't feel right, but couldn't stop. We felt alone and usually mistrusted help when it was offered.

We might have gotten re-infected as young adults trying to fit in or trying to please others or trying to do our patriotic duty. In that effort, some of our basic human values were challenged and then compromised. Our image of what we thought we were doing turned into a nightmare that wouldn't stop. We tried to act 'normal' or tough to hide the pain we were feeling. We were sure no one else could possibly understand what was happening to us.

Those of us who were drafted or enlisted into the armed forces could never have been ready for what we saw and experienced. No matter how tough we thought we were, the **moral injuries** cut the deepest and got us to question our worth; to question whether or not we were even worthy of living.

All of this was loaded into our subconscious body/mind

waiting for a trigger to set off *the memory bombs*. The world we live in has constant new sensations that play with and prey on old memories—thoughts, feelings, and images collected over the years. Understanding these cobwebs and how they influence our actions, can help us have compassion on other people who may do things that appear cruel. We have all done things we wished we had not done. We appreciated the mercy whenever it was shown to us.

So, do we need help? Yes, all of us do. We can't solve our problems and evolve with just our old memories. We need a compassionate listener, new humility and discernment, assurance and hope, understanding and enthusiasm. We can invite more love, joy, peace and courage as guests into our house (mind).

We can look at our 'bad' thoughts and attitudes as symptoms of a plague in our world. (The plague is just trying to survive, too.) We can learn the most by interviewing these thoughts and attitudes. "Where did you come from?" "Why did you pick me?" "When did you first slip into my mind?" "How do you take control of me?" "What are you trying to accomplish?" "Who all do you work with?"

Next, start reprogramming:

> "I am not my thoughts. Yes, my body did things I wish it had never done, but I could not discern the ideas that were controlling me at the time. I thought I was doing the right thing. I was doing the best I could at the time. I forgive myself. **I am not my thoughts**. I have thoughts, but they are not me. I will learn to discern which thoughts to feed and which to starve instead of being a victim of my powerful past. **I forgive myself.**
>
> "I know **if I remain ignorant**, I won't know what to do. **If I doubt** the possibility for positive change, then I won't believe the truth. **If I misunderstand** how to use this knowledge, I won't be able to apply it effectively. **If I am satisfied** with the way I am, I won't have the desire to take charge of my life and change for the better."

"I am <u>not</u> satisfied with my life!
I <u>do</u> desire to change!"

Swimming Hole #5a

Some things to think about:

1. The decision to commit suicide is *the caboose* on the train, the end of a long train of thoughts.
2. Feelings of pain, unloved, left out, condemned, regret, hopeless, not needed, or 'just in somebody else's way' are all fuel for the train.
3. **The more you think upon a thought, the stronger it gets within your mind. Repeat. Repeat. Repeat.**
4. You **can** learn to filter what comes into your mind to keep the plague from completely overtaking you.
5. You **can** learn to filter what comes out of your mouth to keep the plague from using you as a vehicle to hurt or kill someone else.
6. **Do your best not to judge or condemn**; it only feeds the plague.
7. People are not the plague, you are not the plague; the cruel, hateful thoughts and feelings are the viruses that kill the soul.
8. There is **hope**, there is **love**, there is **power** available to charge you up when you're feeling down.
9. There is **knowledge** and **understanding** available to answer your questions and give you direction.
10. There is a **purpose** for your life that you may not yet have dreamed of; *keep searching* until you find it.
11. **Dig for more understanding by asking questions** until the answers make sense.
12. **Don't give up the opportunity to make a better world for all.**

52

Suicides are ravaging various elements of society around the world from farmers in India to veteran and active duty soldiers in the United States. For those of us that have contemplated this action as a possible solution to an overwhelming sense of hopelessness, somehow we found another way out. It may have been a specific person that took time and expressed care for us. It may have been circumstances that changed. It may have been a belief that rose up from the well of our subconscious that shifted our perspective to hope.

Suicide is a word, an idea, a concept that we encounter along life's journey. Usually it takes the suicide of someone we know to get us to focus on what it is. Occasionally, a teacher or minister will introduce us to the term. I believe it is important to challenge the harsh blame and condemnation of suicide victims broadcast by too many Christian ministers.

Let me ask a few questions:

1. Does *God* control everything?
2. Is there a devil?
3. Why do people sin?
4. Does *God* take life?
5. Who/what takes the life of a suicide victim?

Take your time and meditate on these questions; they are very important. Here are some supplemental questions:

- Of course, if *God* is in control of everything, there could be no wrong-doing, no sin, and no free will. If *God* is not in control of everything, what is outside of *God's* control? Does *God* love all of creation?
- If there is a devil, what power does it have? How does the devil exert its power? Is *God* helpless in stopping this devil and its destruction?
- If people sin, they must not be under *God's* control. Are they under the devil's control?
- Does the Lord give life *and* take away life? Did Job's family die at *God's* hand or Satan's hand?
- How can suicide victims be to blame for their own deaths? Who is responsible for passing judgment?
- Does the mercy of the Lord endure forever?

Swimming Hole #5b

Donnie was considered by some "the class clown." For weeks, he had told a few students he was going to bring a gun to school and they laughed it off. He was sitting in the back of his Earth Science class when he pulled a gun out of his book bag, pointed it at himself, and pulled the trigger. All hell broke loose.

The EMTs that transported him to the hospital 30 miles away later reported that Donnie repeatedly said during the trip, "Don't let me die. Don't let me die. Don't let me die." He died shortly after that.

When they pulled up at the spot over-looking the lake early that evening, they were calm. He got out and said he'd be right back for one of her delicious cookies. He got the hose out of the trunk, attached it to the exhaust pipe, fed it through the slightly opened back window, and got back in. The car was running with a full tank.

"How about one of those cookies? I'll read you your favorite poem. 'How do I love thee? Let me count the ways. I love you more than...'."

They were found dead the next morning. They were in their early 80s and had been fairly healthy. They had lost friends and family members and had watched as most got sick, went into hospitals, and had expensive tests and treatments that only extended their lives briefly. Huge medical bills fell on the survivors.

This couple decided to die with dignity before a major illness put them in the same situation. They 'got their house in order' and planned the details of how and where they would do it.

Robin Williams was a very successful actor/performer who depended on his sharp mental acuity. After the shock of his suicide, it was discovered that he had been suffering at least a year from Lewy Body Dementia—he was literally losing his mind. He was aware that it was happening, but he never knew the cause of it. He sought help from many medical and lifestyle professionals, but it continued to get worse. No one knew until later that there was nothing that could have helped him.

6.

The Judging Virus Epidemic

What 'ologists' are studying

the Judging Virus epidemic?

Copyright © 2015 Value Life Associates

Judging People

Some of us remember going through our day, riding the teeter-totter of superior-inferior feelings. From waking up to falling asleep, we were better-than or worse-than the varied people we encountered face-to-face or simply in our imaginations. We had no control over this daily ride; it defined and redefined how we saw ourselves. We had no idea these feelings were symptoms of being infected with the **judging virus**.

Yes, I'm comparing this common, damaging habit of **judging**, to common viruses (e.g. HSV, HPV, flu, chicken pox, HIV). Viruses are encapsulated pieces of genetic information carried to their target cells where they attach and replicate to do their damage and spread. Scientists are studying how to control these physical viruses. NOTE: You are NOT the virus! Often there is sympathy for those infected with a physical virus.

The judging virus is a *meme*, an expression of cultural information, spread by social intercourse, and infecting at least 99.9% of humanity. The medical profession seems helpless to address this pandemic. A few in the social sciences are developing and using tools such as *Cognitive Replacement Therapy* and *Cognitive Reframing* to address it. Many church leaders simply say,

"Don't judge." REMEMBER: You are NOT the judging virus!

How does one get infected? A child is not born with the **judging virus**, but those around the newborn **are** infected and contagious in varying degrees. We call them a host (like a hotel) and a vector when they transmit it. This **judging virus**, like all viruses, does not care who you are or who it judges. It lives and multiples by being active in the host's mind and being communicated to others.

Whether spoken or by body language, the **judging virus** infects very young children. Harsh words and actions of an infected person hit a child's sensory receptors and penetrate its unprotected mind. "Shut up! Stop crying!" Slap! Somewhat surprisingly, praise can also pass the **virus** to the child. "You are so much sweeter than your brother!" Zap!

Once inside the new host, the **judging virus** takes control of how they see themselves and others. It behaves like a self-right, superior quick-draw judge, condemning or praising both its host and those viewed by the host.

The **judging virus** is a **belief**. "I am _____." Just fill in words that sound to you like superior or inferior statements. Often, they include "better than" and "worse than" because they are always comparing. "...but they, measuring themselves by themselves and comparing themselves among themselves, are not wise." (2Co.10:12) This has been a problem for millennia.

Throughout its life, the **judging virus** continues to condemn or praise its host and those viewed by its host whenever there is opportunity, even when no one else is around. The **judging virus** simply reminds the host of how stupid/smart or clumsy/talented or unwanted/important they are in relation to others. Are you sensitive to criticism? The range of negative consequences of being criticized goes from hurt and depression to death.

Yes, this **judging virus** in the child or adult is highly contagious and takes full advantage of opportunities to spread to whoever is in earshot or on social media. 'Bullying' has pushed some to suicide. Unfortunately, the 'bully' then gets condemned (bullied) and no one learns anything. **Bullying** others and self-blame are two sides of the same coin. A person can only **bully** you if they have been **bullied** or observed a significant other **bully** someone. In either scenario, they get infected with the **judging virus**.

Radio, television, movies and social media are constantly feeding and spreading **judging viruses**. No wonder it's a pandemic. Competition is all about winners and losers. It is common for winners to swell with pride and superior thoughts. It is common for losers to shrink with shame and inferior thoughts. Both point fingers. As you may have heard for years, "When you point a condemning finger at someone, three other fingers are pointing at you." (as on the card)

This judging pandemic stirs up wars and every other form of violence. Infected leaders and their mouthpiece media demonize people as a justification for killing them or treating them inhumanely. The **judging virus** *meme* is that powerful.

> *"The Judging Virus*
> *has done more to injure and kill people,*
> *to separate and destroy relationships,*
> *and to rob people of their health and happiness,*
> *than any other single cause."* DD

We need to figure this **judging virus** out; all murders, suicides, and wars are caused by it. Whenever we observe the **judging virus** using us toward others, we are beginning to separate the soul from its thoughts and actions; the more we 'catch' it, the faster we can insert the effective substitute, and stop behaving like a *meme-machine* inwardly and a broadcaster of our **judging virus**.

A Personal Example

I was pulled over by our local police at 11:30 one January night in 2007 after I did a rolling stop before turning onto a deserted street (he was parked—lights off). The two times he engaged me through my open window, **a deep rage of words and emotions spewed out of my mouth** (for the first time in my life). While it was very intense, it was not personal (I didn't know him) nor vulgar (I don't store foul language). The only line I recall from the two encounters is, "It's situations like this that send people to the hospital!" He calmly asked if I wanted him to escort me to the nearest hospital and I shouted, "NO!"

For weeks, I told my story to family, friends, and students in my classes. I believed the police were *so* wrong and I was *so* right and ready to fight it. On court day, my students advised me to pay the fine. I did, but I continued to rant and rail.

Finally, standing in front of my class one day, I had one of those 2-by-4 revelations: "I am a health teacher and this self-righteous anger is hurting me and those I pass it on to." I knew immediately **I needed to discern the source** of this anger. Having done this many times on other issues in the past, the source quickly became clear.

For nearly twenty years, Black students had shared reports of being pulled over for DWB (Driving While Black). Growing up as an underdog in my neighborhood, I sided with my Black students and judged the local police as bad people. Each time I judged them, I was quietly feeding an **angry wolf** in my heart (See Chapter 12). By the time **I** was pulled over (on the same street so many of my students were stopped), that **angry wolf** had grown huge and was overpowering. **I** was **not** in control.

With this diagnosis and the source identified, I knew from earlier training that I was a ***prisoner*** and I needed help. I recalled a friend's email telling the story of a Hawaiian psychiatrist and his "I'm sorry, I love you" practice known as ***Ho'oponopono***.

When I first read it months before, I dismissed it as too far out. In this new circumstance, I decided to apply it religiously each time I saw or thought about the police and each time that night flashed back out of my subconscious. I knew I had been infected with the self-right/condemning **judging virus**. I needed to forgive the police (I'm sorry, I love you) and my **Self** (I'm sorry, I love you).

Within four weeks I felt healed. To me, that meant I no longer had an emotional stir when I remembered that event and the many events that led up to it. I did not blame or condemn anyone, including myself, for what transpired. It was all about forgiveness.

Forgiveness

Forgiveness is a decision to **substitute** one belief for another. A **judging virus** gets us to believe we are superior or inferior to others. To forgive, we **substitute** a different belief. This is mine:

*"I am no better or worse
than any other soul.*

*I cannot judge
that any individual
is in full control of its
thoughts and actions
at any particular time.* " DD

You may recall an old expression: "I love you, but I don't like what you did." The mother separated the soul from the act. That is a requirement in forgiving! Separate you, the soul, from your actions; separate the other soul's appearance or actions from them.

The Shack by William P. Young is a novel (and now a movie) about judging and forgiveness. A man who had killed his own father as a teenager loses his youngest daughter to a serial killer. He meets *God* (in three persons) while in a coma from a car accident and learns that *God* forgives all people for every action—no exceptions. Why? *God* sees each developing moment of each soul's life and understands what causes it to behave for better or for worse and *God* forgives the worse. That is true love. Is your *God* like this or does your *God* judge and condemn?

Most Christians grow up hearing and reciting a prayer known as the Lord's prayer (Mat.6:9-12): "... And forgive us our debts [sins, trespasses] as we forgive our debtors [those that have sinned or trespassed against us] ...". One disciple asked how many times should he forgive; seven times? Jesus said, "Seventy times seven." (Mat.18:21-22) This was a brand-new message to hear: **never stop forgiving**. By the way, do those you forgive need to first confess to you and beg your forgiveness? I don't think so. Does your *God* require you to confess and beg forgiveness before you are forgiven? Hmm?

As a point of explanation, I keep saying "your *God*" because everyone perceives their *God* uniquely. I agree with psychiatrist Carl Jung who believed we each create our own image of *God* and the image is never accurate. When someone asks me if I believe in *God*, I may ask, "Which *God*?" Or I may say, "I believe in love and the Bible says, "*God* is love," so I guess I believe in *God*." I put *God* in italics to make that point.

Until you have the revelation that you are not your thoughts, you can be manipulated by the widespread propaganda that labels and condemns people. **You**, the individual observer, **are not** superior or inferior; Black, Brown, Red, Yellow, or White; male, hermaphrodite, or female; rich or poor. **You** are a unique, indivisible being, a pod of consciousness that presently has a body that gets you around, beliefs you look through to see the world, and feelings that get associated with your beliefs and your relationships.

I highly recommend *Forgiveness: A Bold Choice for a Peaceful Heart* by Robin Casarjian. I heard her speak at a **National Wellness Conference** and resonated with each word. She separates the **Self** from its *pain body* (the consequence of being infected by the **judging virus**). We are a prisoner to the *pain* as long as the **judging virus** is living in our minds. Getting rid of the *pain* and out of prison is a process of forgiveness. The last statement in her book:

> "We are given opportunity after opportunity to learn the lessons of love. We are given the knowledge of forgiveness to assure our success. In a world where there is much fear, we are given all the boldness that is needed to live out our purpose as teachers of love."

Consequences

This is a good place to discuss consequences since so many people are conditioned to rationalize their self-right **judging virus** and demand consequences. Does your perception (and therefore emotion) change when you learn someone's behavior is due to a sickness or handicap rather than an act of intentionality?

The shift in perception is because we see they were likely not in control of their behavior. How far can we extend that? At what point can we say, "They should be punished because I know they did it on purpose. Of course, they are in control of their actions!" **How could we possibly have that inside information?**

This starts with very young children. How do we know for sure what they understand about themselves and the world around them? Do we understand them? If we are still infected with the **judging virus**, we don't even understand ourselves.

So much of what we perceive and do is a result of tradition. Why do we send our children to a school that demands they sit on hard chairs in regimented classrooms and obey the teacher who requires them to learn thus and such in a certain way at a certain pace? Does that meet the needs and desires of the student or the needs and desires of a capitalistic, factory-based economy?

Do we want creative children excited with learning what their unique gifts and talents are or do we want good test grades based on some imaginary standard of what smart looks like? Do we want narrowly indoctrinated children that are ignorant to the beautiful diversity of life and culture in this world? Or do we want children growing up appreciating the rich diversity of life and culture?

Overbearing requirements on a child have consequences. When their elders are stuck in **culturally inhumane traditions** of self-right judgment, the consequences are toxic and can be deadly for the children who grow up and pass the traditions on to their children. Maybe cultures need to go through a re-evaluation and rebirth when their traditions are inhumane.

I am encouraging you to examine the world between your ears and its culture so you won't continue to rain **terror** on others. Do you want to act like a **terrorist** stirring fear in others? Do you want **indoctrinated judging** to be the motivator for your behavior and the behaviors of your children? I really hope you don't.

Judgment Day

Jesus said, "Judge not, that you be not judged." (Mat.7:1) Most Christians are taught there's a future day when all will stand before the seat of judgment. In the parable of the sheep and goats which many connect to a judgment day (Mat.26:31-46 NLT), Jesus says,

> And the King will say, I tell you the truth, when you did it to one of the least of these my brothers and sisters, you were doing it to me!

If you are a Christian, I ask, "What if you really believed that whatever you do to or for every other person on this earth, you are doing to or for Jesus?" He did want you to seriously consider that possibility, didn't he? I'm not saying this to send you on a guilt trip; I'm encouraging you to re-examine your relationships.

So, as we examine each idea, each new and old belief, we ask if it is true, if it is promoting health, if it is loving? Does it make the world a better place for all? This inquiry takes time and possibly a neutral, compassionate listener. Those who do not trust a person with their stories can use a notebook or speak to their *God*. You are **not** saying that you're a bad person; you are acknowledging the bad ideas (***viral memes***) that have used your mind and body.

Judgment Day could easily be a metaphor for everyday that the **judging virus** continues to live and control the way we see ourselves and others. **Let's do away with judgment day!** Let's replace the **judging virus** belief with the truth that no one soul is any better or any worse than any other soul.

"Judge not, that you be not judged" could mean, that as long as you are the host for a **judging virus**, it will continue to judge you and all those around you. When you do away with the **judging virus**, it won't be judging you or others anymore. That's victory. That's overcoming. That's Christ-like. For you ex-Christians or non-Christians reading this, I think you get the point of the message without having to use *God* or Jesus or the Bible.

It is time to look at history, the present, and the future through new glasses—glasses that don't condemn, blame, and judge. It is so powerful to go back through your own life and see that you and others were doing the best you could while "shackled with emotional chains wrought by dysfunctional behaviors, programmed by the stories of the past." If you have not yet had the revelation that you are not your thoughts, if will be difficult to see those of your past are not their thoughts. I trust the revelation will come in due time.

Swimming Hole #6a

This is a story from the 2001 **National Wellness Conference** in Stevens Point, Wisconsin. Of the many breakout sessions offered, I was drawn to one conducted by Jean Houston, the morning keynote.

Several hundred, mostly younger women, were in attendance and Dr. Houston led us through a variety of *exercises* to help us focus on areas of ourselves that we might have overlooked in the past. One such *exercise* had us list roles we've played in our lives. She indicated we were not schizophrenic, but *polyphrenic* — shifting from one role to another throughout the day: son, father, teacher, husband, cook, recycler, singer, dancer, minister, and so on.

A couple of volunteers were sought who shared their lists. Afterwards, she called on my raised hand: "Were we supposed to list only the *good* roles we've played? What about our *dark* or *shadow* roles?" Immediately, she had us list our *shadow* characters. She asked, "Is anyone willing to share one of their *shadows*?" Ten or so folks, including me, raised our hands. She called on me.

"Please tell us what it is." "I've had some voyeur bouts with pornography." "Okay, just stand over there while I *look* at you." After 20 seconds or so, she said, "I'm going to tell you the essence of your *shadow*. It is the hierophant (def. a priest of ancient Greece who interpreted sacred mysteries). The more you engage in the role of hierophant, its *shadow* side will have less impetus to manifest."

She did not condemn my *shadow*. Without honestly acknowledging my *shadow*, I would not have learned about the gift of its flip side. Think how many in the world are controlled by a *shadow* aspect of their unrecognized essence.

Don't condemn. Look for the flip side.

Swimming Hole #6b

Rewriting the Story

With the knowledge you now have, that...

1. the soul is separate from its thoughts,
2. people grow up a prisoner of culture,
3. a judging virus has infected each of us, and
4. we can replace old beliefs with new ones,

you can go back through your history and the history of humanity during the last 10,000 years and see it through a different paradigm (pair of glasses). Nearly all those souls behaved as unskilled victims attempting to survive and solve the problems of the day.

Just because a few woke up beyond the victim stage does not make the rest guilty of some fault. Just because messages of love, kindness, and mercy were shared did not mean people had the necessary skill to put those attitudes into practice.

You can now have compassion on yourself struggling in the past and all those people you hear about and read about. We were all doing the best we could with the tools made available to us. The vast majority of the seven billion people in the world today are handicapped by the **judging virus** and are not yet able to replace it.

As you and others begin to see the past differently and can forgive all those in the past that had been condemned, you are re-writing his-story and her-story. As the people of the past are forgiven, there is more hope for the future and you are better able to respond to all you see and hear with clearer vision and greater wisdom.

A shift is in the works; a paradigm shift. Judging has only brought hurt and separation. Forgiveness will heal and bring us together. Do you have a choice?

If it is to be, it is up to US!

7.

Consciousness – What do you control?

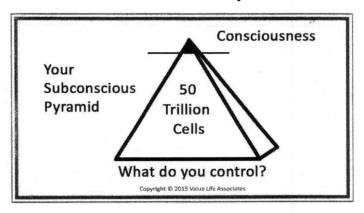

Consciousness

What are you **conscious** of right now? This morning as I sat in my car waiting for my cat at the vets, I made a list of what I was conscious of (aware of). Sight and hearing had most of my attention. Third was my body touching the seat and arm rest; then a taste of the coffee I recently finished. I started noticing thoughts fluttering in and out: images, memories, ideas, projected imaginations. When I would focus on any one thing, I lost consciousness of the others.

What we notice (are conscious of) is less than 5% of our total cognitive activity. The rest of our mind (100 billion neurons) and body (50 trillion cells) operate subconsciously. You might have read about this in Marianne Szegedy-Maszak's article, *"Mysteries of the mind: Your unconscious is making your everyday decisions,"* in US News and World Report in 2005. *"Unconscious"* (as the noun) and *"subconscious"* have the same meaning (i.e. without or below consciousness).

Memories and **imaginations** stream up like playful dolphins from our **subconscious**. Past and future are painted with lingering brush strokes; some are 'photographed' and stored. Pause for a minute or two and see what stream of **consciousness** flows from the image of *pyramids* or *playful dolphins*. That stream flows from your **subconscious**, stays a moment, and returns. No problem. Right? It is an amazing database that researchers are working to understand more about every day.

Let's start at our beginnings and explore consciousness. Were the sperm and egg **conscious** (awake or aware) before they conceived your body? No. They behaved as robot delivery machines, unable to observe or make decisions; each carrying a cargo of genetic information. Is a zygote (all cells identical) or blastocyst (specialized cells up to implantation) conscious of their journey down the fallopian tube or, in rare cases, down into the abdominal cavity? No.

How about an embryo anchored in the womb until all its body parts are present? Those who oppose abortion talk as if a conscious **Self** is housed in the uterus. There certainly is an organized collection of living cells, tissues, and organs being nourished by the nutrients from the umbilical cord and the beginning nervous system of receptor and motor neurons. The embryo body does react to its environment, but not as a **Self**-aware or **Self**-conscious being. Just because an organism has an emotional expression of pain, does not mean there is a **Self** to be aware of it. The same could be said for the fetus through to full-term.

Unique mixtures of genes and gene expression give character to this developing human organism. The electromagnetic and biochemical actions and reactions are undeniable, but no **Self** is yet there. I have come to believe that until an organism is **Self**-aware or **Self**-conscious, it is nothing more than an amazing body receiving millions of sensory messages and displaying consequent pre-programmed reactions. Cells do what they are built to do. [If I have pushed a hot button in your worldview, I consider it a good sign and encourage you to explore how the button got built into your subconscious and is now beyond your control.]

From conception on, every single experience of this precious new living product becomes part of its **subconscious** body-mind. At the same time, those **Self**-aware people that are thinking about this developing baby create their personal image of the **Self/Soul** of the baby. Once born, they give it names and traits, histories and dreams, and a lot of their personal projections. The baby receives this repetitious flood of information through its available senses.

Then, sometime around the age of two, most toddlers have a

realization, often while seeing themselves in the mirror, "*I am the one in the mirror. I am the one they are all talking about.*" The **Self**, that was first created in the minds of those around the baby and transmitted via social intercourse to the baby, becomes **conscious** in a flash of revelation.

"The pre-frontal cortex
has birthed its Self—
the first level of Self-awareness." DD

> "American Indian lore speaks of three miracles. The first miracle is that anything exists at all. The second miracle is that living things exist. The third miracle is that living things exist that *know* they exist. As human beings conscious of ourselves, we represent the third miracle."
>
> Duane Elgin in his book *The Living Universe*

Self can go to sleep and, during REM sleep, its subconscious plays in its dreams. **Self** is either unconscious or has very limited consciousness during sleep. In a vegetative state, the **Self** is less than asleep, it is unwired—gone. A coma can be two or more options. One is much more like sleep when the **Self** is present, but **not aware** or **conscious**. Another is like a person in the operating room who has been given some anesthesia and a muscle relaxant before an operation; if there's not enough anesthesia, the **Self** can be aware and experience emotions and sensations, but not express reactions.

Near-death experiences sometimes demonstrate how the **Self** can become a wireless **pod of consciousness** that leaves the confines of the physical body. The **Self** is still aware, but uses a kind of **remote viewing**. Once in this wireless mode, the **Self** is free of time and space, and can be anywhere. This was depicted in *The Shack*, a novel by William P. Young. Some people have learned to go wireless and have out-of-body experiences. See Chapter 17 for more examples.

Some have experienced orbs as **pods of consciousness** and some have spoken to these **pods of consciousness** telepathically.

The variety of paranormal experiences is phenomenal. We have so much more to learn and I believe those that poo-poo the paranormal are demonstrating their personal biases and limitations.

Control

It's a huge issue in our lives. Just take a moment and brainstorm as many ways **control** or lack of **control** plays a role in your sense of security. "Out of control" often stirs anxiety; "under control" seems to calm us. As you process this section, monitor your anxious/calm barometer and note what gets triggered when.

In my **Personal and Community Health** classes, one of the three 1000-word written paper assignments included a section on their philosophy of life. Here is one of the six questions:

> Who or what controls your thoughts and actions (gets you to do things you don't want to do)?

In Chapter Two I asked you, *"Do you ever do things you don't want to do?"* Do you remember your answer? Please take a moment and answer that first philosophy question?

I believe **control** is a bigger issue than most might ever have imagined. Among thousands of answers, there were two camps—the majors (1) and the minors (2):

1. *Nobody controls me but me;* and
2. *I am greatly influenced by my environment (e.g. people important to me, peers, weather).*

Another question relates to **control**, without using the term:

> Do people have day-to-day freedom of choice or is our future already predetermined by childhood experiences or by a *God*?

Again, I encourage you to take a moment and respond. You may wonder why this is even in a college health class. Here's why: If one truly believes their future is predetermined (not in their control), they will not feel a personal sense of responsibility for their future. That belief also goes hand-in-hand with the much-used phrase, *"Everything happens for a reason."* Why learn about taking charge of your life when you believe it is all up to your *God*?

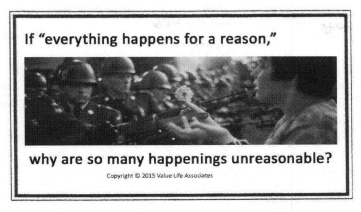

If "everything happens for a reason,"

why are so many happenings unreasonable?

Copyright © 2015 Value Life Associates

Many students have expressed an oxymoron (competing *memes*): "*I have **free** will <u>and</u> God **determines** my life.*" They also think these two **beliefs** are compatible. They say, "*God gives us free will, but already knows what we will choose.*" It is not uncommon to have two opposing **beliefs** residing in our minds at the same time (e.g. a **belief** that it is wrong to lie and a **belief** that rationalizes lying).

Here is my ~~free~~ *will* speech from the Preface: "Society does not like to think they are slaves of a master. Society likes to hold up the banner of **free will** and **personal responsibility** as though everyone has always had it. I contend up front that **our will is never *free***. We each have a will, but it is constantly influenced and/or manipulated by the powers of competing *memes* inside and outside each mind."

The Automated Body/Mind

This *Pyramid* card was inspired by some points Bruce Lipton made in his ***Biology of Belief*.** We do not control the vast majority of the 30-50 trillion cells that make up our bodies. The identical genetic codes of DNA within the nucleus of each cell are the repositories of infinite possibilities, but, as Bruce says, "The brain of the cell is the membrane which is loaded with unique proteins that respond to the constantly changing environment."

The science of **Epigenetics** has revealed how each organism's environment continually modifies its genetic code (e.g. switches genes or parts of genes off and on). That environment includes people, food, water, air, electro-magnetic forces, temperature, **and thoughts**. From conception, every protein, molecule, cell, and system has responded and adapted to its ever-changing environment. Significant habits developed and all of this has been without and beyond our **control**.

We get programmed with the language and culture of those around us. Punishment and reward establish powerful patterns. The abundance or lack of love in our childhoods set up almost uncontrollable drives throughout our lives. Much of the time, we have no idea why we can't control certain urges—both helpful and harmful. We are dominated by the notions of peers and elders with little awareness of who or what we are. Why did the seemingly successful high school football star commit suicide? No one had a clue.

What Can We Control?

I find it interesting that humans do a better job of 'controlling' others through intimidation and indoctrination than in controlling themselves. They fail to realize *why* they do what they do partly because they are so completely wired with previously established body/mind habits that it feels impossible to separate those habits from the **Self**. Muscle memory and emotional memory dictate pre-programmed behaviors without them even being conscious of the possibility of choice.

By age four I was lying to my mother with a straight face. When I got to grade school, I had one brief interaction with the janitor who let me know I could choose to stop lying. I made a choice to stop lying. I did not master that *meme* immediately, but from then on, I knew I had a choice.

The second choice I recall was a result of hitting a bird with a BB shortly after getting a BB gun. The bird flopped around and I panicked. I ended its suffering with a big rock. I felt horrible. I made a little cross. I decided never to use or carry a gun again.

Of the millions of packets of sensory input and trillions of branch signals they trigger each second, **a personal decision becomes a precious act of will.** The opportunity we have to make a personal decision is less than one-in-a-billion of the 'decisions' our body-mind makes every second of every day. It is hard to remember that the vast majority of sensory-motor behaviors are not conscious personal decisions—they are pre-programmed reactions.

What Controls Us?

Our cultural programming came from caregivers (e.g. parents, teachers, baby-sitters, daycare staff, older siblings, friends, books, TV and other digital sources provided to us). Happiness, security, and feeling loved made us feel good and we intrinsically 'like' those feelings. We continually adapt to those around us to recapture the pleasure of those feelings. If we didn't feel loved in relationships, we may find that **heroin—the love drug**—fills that biochemical void.

Our identity comes from caregivers and is subject to change. We may have one identity with grandma, one with the daycare staff, another with Mom that may not be the same as with Dad. We are constantly in survival mode and do our very best not to get hurt.

As our bodies change, our clothes change, our feelings change, the way people treat us changes and we continue to adapt. Through all of this, we create safety zones as best we can. For some, it may be a room or outdoors area; for others, it may be a 'cigar box' or a notebook. Some kids develop a special talent or appear to enjoy 'an imaginary friend'. Some even develop an alternate personality to escape their pain.

Sometime in their youth, huge options get presented (e.g. sex, drugs, work, religion, education, babies). Some very young adults are told, "This is your life; what are you going to do with it?" All their past, stored in their body/mind, starts talking. What a parent wants may win. Underneath all the chatter, there is a search going on; a search for the 'authentic' **Self**.

I highly recommend books and presentations by Dr. Gabor Mate, a compassionate physician who has worked with many people struggling with addictions. I used his book, ***In the Realm of Hungry Ghosts***, in my Drug Education classes.

71

Four Levels of the Psyche

Jean Houston is a pioneer and leader in developing tools to enhance human capacities toward becoming *The Possible Human* in *The Possible Society*. Her research led to hundreds of exercises to expand and deepen what she calls the *Four Levels of the Psyche* or Awareness:

> L1 = Physical/Sensory
> L2 = Historical/Psychological
> L3 = Mythic/Symbolic
> L4 = Unitive/Integral

Jean has spoken of these four levels around the world to many cultures. People are taught how to access these levels at will. I am adding the element of **Self**: the observant, willful soul. **I** observe or focus on what attracts or distracts my attention. Despite the passionate testimony of those who text while driving, they will be focusing on texting or driving, not both at the same time.

The goal of the *Four Levels of the Psyche* is to expand what is *attractive* to us to give us greater access to actualize our potentials as human beings. Jean calls it, "cooking on more burners." We have so much potential physically, mentally, mythically, and spiritually that has not been actualized.

Briefly, **L1** seems animalistic, yet us human animals can intentionally expand our physical and sensory powers. In **L2**, we learn of our amazing histories and powers of the mind with its ever-increasing possibilities. We are moved by music, art in all its forms, and empathy for others. **L3** teaches us to step into a whole new level of powers by seeing our inner and outer worlds through the lens of symbolism and mythic stories. In **L4** we see that we all live in relationship to the entirety of existence, that the whole is greater than the sum of its parts, and that love can transcend **Self**. We experience what it is like to swim in the fullness of the living Universe.

I've been guided through the Four Levels exercise many times. The most memorable was led by Peggy Rubin during a 2002 Mystery School weekend. Peggy asked us to pick an animal that we wanted to *be* as we moved through the Four Levels. I picked a turtle.

In the ***Physical/Sensory level***, I imagined slowly moving about sniffing for scents, keenly listening, feeling subtle movements of the earth, tasting the tidbits I nibbled on, and seeing in detail the limited area available to me in the grass.

As she guided us into the ***Historical/Psychological level***, I could now remember my turtle genealogy and the embankment where I was born and to which I returned each year. I recalled how sad I felt at seeing cousins caught defenseless on the streets and highways as careless speeding drivers crushed them.

As Peggy then called forth the ***Mythic/Symbolic level***, I suddenly grew wings and started to fly. It was thrilling to soar over the land and sea and even back in time over other lands. I could see the amazing diversity of turtles everywhere I looked. I loved being a **Flying Turtle**.

Then she gently shifted us into the ***Unitive/Integral level*** and I marveled at the sense of oneness I felt, not only with other turtles, but with the Earth and all its varied inhabitants. This sense of unity swelled out through the solar system, the galaxy, the Universe, to the realm of the Great Turtles that birthed it all.

I didn't want this feeling to end when I heard,

> "Know in your being that you can learn to move fluidly through these Four Levels of awareness from moment to moment. To see yourself and the world through these glasses, grants you new powers of perception, playfulness, and appreciation."

A few months after that delicious experience, I participated in a **New Warrior Training Adventure Weekend**. In the course of *that* deep, transformative three days, we were asked to pick a totem name for ourselves. It may come as no surprise that the totem name I claimed was ***Flying Turtle***.

As I type these words, a multicolored turtle kite flies suspended above my head and my awareness flows through the *Four Levels*. Pine forest incense burns, a rainforest white-noise machine sounds, coffee is close by, I feel the floor and the keyboard. Photos and artifacts of family and friends, my mother's large mirror, *god*s and *goddesses* surround me. Every atom here is five billion years old with hydrogen as its thirteen billion-year-old grandmother that came from Spirit that infuses everything. Wow! I am deeply grateful.

Swimming Hole #7

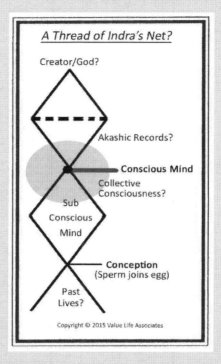

A Thread of Indra's Net?

Creator/God?

Akashic Records?

Conscious Mind

Collective Consciousness?

Sub Conscious Mind

Conception (Sperm joins egg)

Past Lives?

Copyright © 2015 Value Life Associates

Sometime in our first few years of life, we become a **Self** and consciously communicate with the very few humans we encounter.

Who am I? Am I here on a mission? What is my purpose? Some believe past lives are influencing what they are here to do. Some believe their *God* talks to them. Others believe they have been or can be in contact with the Collective Consciousness (Universal Mind, Akashic Records, Cosmic Consciousness), angels or extra-terrestrials.

As one of seven billion individuals on the planet receiving more information in one day than any generation in known human history, you struggle to make sense of the relatively small amount you are able to process. All the stored information in your subconscious body/mind adds enormously to the questions and to the answers.

8.

Do you have any Misconceptions?

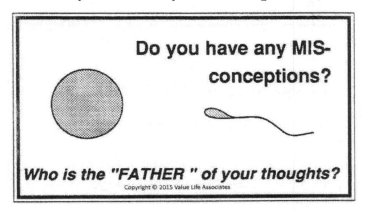

How do we acquire and develop our beliefs? Why are people's beliefs so similar and yet so unique? One way to explain the answer is through the use of one of my favorite analogies.

In a college speech class, I learned that communication could be described as *social intercourse* and that much of our language of communication paralleled the language of sexual intercourse. We artificially in*seminate* an egg or a female and we dis*seminate* ideas or information. We *conceive* babies and we *conceive* ideas. An offspring's *body* grows in the womb of the female and a *body* of knowledge grows in the mind of the learner.

This parallel language showed up again in my Bible study classes during ministerial training. *God* was referred to as "Father" when acting as the source of holy messages (Joh.12:49; 14:24). The devil was referred to as the "father" of evil messages (Joh.8:38-44).

In my **Personal and Community Health** classroom, this Parable Card was rolled out as a soon coming Whisper Quiz. You will not be quizzed, but you may find yourself talking softly to others about the message. Here is the 'Big Picture' I would draw piece-by-piece on the chalkboard.

An Analogy

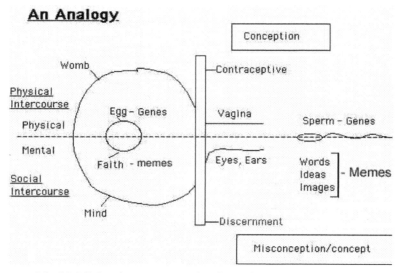

To highlight the power and value of **Analogies**, I relate my story of applying to graduate school at Mizzou and being required to take the *Miller's Analogies* test to qualify for acceptance. Thankfully, I did well enough. Here is an example from one of their promo booklets. See how you do.

Salt is related to Hypertension as Sugar is related to
   a. cholesterol
   b. carbohydrates
   c. hyperthyroidism
   d. diabetes.

That was almost too easy; I'm sure you picked "d." Now let's apply this to the picture. We could say,

Conception : Misconception :: Physical Intercourse :
   a. mind
   b. eyes
   c. Social Intercourse
   d. discernment.

You are on a roll.

The *Conception* of a baby is by way of *Physical Intercourse*; a *Misconception or Concept* is the result of *Social Intercourse*. I would ask the class, "Who played the male role in social intercourse during the last week?" A couple of guys might raise their hands. Just as the phrase 'social intercourse' was new to me in college, it was also new to most of them. They quickly realized they all had played that role again and again.

Conception of a baby can be prevented by using a *Contraceptive* or maintaining abstinence. To keep a *Concept or Misconception* from conceiving in our minds, we must first build and then use a filter of *Discernment* or else avoid certain communications.

Do you have any misconceptions? Undoubtedly; we all do. A misconception is simply a wrong idea or misunderstanding about something. It may be difficult to recognize ones we have right this minute, but we can all look back and identify a few from the past. I actually asked my students to give me a list of the four or five most common misconceptions children get before the age of five. Their consistent list each semester for over thirty years has been: Santa Claus, Easter Bunny, Tooth Fairy and Boogie Man. The Stork is also popular.

Who is the 'Father' of your thoughts? Remember, I am not talking gender here. In ***Social Intercourse,*** some person or organization *sends* a message (male role) and someone else *receives* the message (female role). So, who do you think originated the wrong ideas that later wound up conceiving in our children's **Minds?** Students generally list parents, TV, and society as their big three. Where did they get those messages to send? They are really just messengers passing on what someone had passed to them.

Do infants have a choice as to what messages to accept and which to keep out? How about a one-year-old? Two? Three? We are built to accept all the messages that come in through our senses until such a time when our accumulated experiences and ideas are able to organize a discernment filter to keep other ideas out. It is a process that can continue throughout life.

To dig into this a little further, remember that our parents were once children receiving messages from their elders, as has been the case with every generation. ***Memes*** (ideas) get passed from mind to mind through *Social Intercourse* starting shortly after we come out of the womb. A baby senses body language, tone of voice, and stress levels of people in close proximity and reacts appropriately—even if it doesn't understand why it is behaving the way it is.

This book is not about blame, it's about understanding. Let's understand how and why we think what we think, feel what we feel, believe what we believe, and do what we do. Thoughts conceive in our minds when messages are received and we believe them. Children accept messages easily because they haven't formed a **Discernment** filter to shield them. They have no **Contraceptive of the Mind** until it gets built.

Tradition is the most common cause of passing along **Misconceptions**. *"That's the way my parents raised me." "We've always done it that way."* When we have not taken the time to examine the origins and possible, broader consequences of some of these traditions, we just follow suit.

Misconceptions are not limited to childhood stories. All conflicts in the world started by way of the same process described above. To clearly understand what someone's communication is *intended* to mean is close to impossible.

Because each of us experiences life differently and, therefore, perceives life differently, we hear the messages of others through our own complex and unique discernment filter. We also speak out through a slightly different filter based on what we want the listener to hear. We can speak sincerely, we can act as deceitful manipulators, or we can perform as 'robots' of tradition.

The Parents who cried, "Wolf!"

"Grandma, is there really a Jesus Christ and a God?"

Copyright © 2015 Value Life Associates

Let me read it again: The **Parents** who cried, "Wolf!" Sit with it for a few minutes. This card represents a true story that I've repeated to every class I've taught since 1981:

I was teaching a ***Stress Management*** series in eight weeks to a local Methodist Church Sunday school class of 120 parents and grandparents. The seventh week, on holiday stress, they were sure I had called them liars for teaching their kids to believe in Santa Claus. They put up an invisible wall. I internally panicked, felt like a fast-paddling duck on water wondering what I should do next.

Just then, an elder woman stood and turned to the class:

> I want to tell you what happened this year with my granddaughter. She came to me and said, "Grandma, Mommy and Daddy said there was a Santa Claus and there really wasn't. Then they said there was an Easter Bunny and there really wasn't. And they told me there was a Tooth Fairy and there really wasn't. Now they're telling me there's a Jesus Christ and a God. Grandma, is there really a Jesus Christ and a God?"

She sat down. The room was quiet. I had big goose bumps. The wall melted. We moved on to other holiday stresses. That story was one of the most profound teachings I've ever received.

It took me a few years more to realize the parallel to **the boy who cried wolf**, but when *that* revelation came, it made the story even more powerful. I am so grateful for that grandmother.

In response to students saying little kids are 'dumb', a young mother in one of my college health classes stood and told what had happened with her three-year-old the previous year.

> We had just left Santa's Workshop at the Mall and turned at Center Court into another wing. My daughter saw another Santa and asked, "Mommy, who is that?" I swallowed hard and said, "Oh, that's Santa's helper." She looked up at me and said, "Mommy, that's a lie."

Put yourself in that mother's situation; what would you have said? *That three-year-old* had developed her own unique **discernment filter** that would not accept that lie. The girl had seen the movies and other media depicting Santa and Santa's helpers. She *knew* the difference. Mommy was busted.

Too often we think our children are our playthings. The fact is, they are listening, watching, taking it all in as if it was true. They don't have discernment until they piece it together from our example and messages and the messages of others.

Kids love to pretend. I had taught my daughter that Santa was a pretend character like Superman. On his kids show at Christmas, a local TV celebrity looked out at my daughter and said, "*Kids, if your parents are saying there is no Santa Claus, they're lying to you!*" What to do? Be a hypocrite and lie? Who do we want our kids to trust?

Yes, it is difficult to be truthful when a whole culture supports a tradition of lies and misconceptions, but there are healthy alternatives. Let your kids in on the fun. Have the whole family make presents; dress up as Santa, his family and helpers; and take the presents to people less fortunate. **It will be a win-win-win for all**. Is it more blessed to give or to covet a long list of material things? Which lesson do you want your child to internalize?

Swimming Hole #8

In today's world, as old traditions are being challenged again, stubborn resistance again fights back. We don't realize we were all raised with the misconception that people *are* their thoughts and actions. Many old traditions are just stagnant *memes* acting out over and over.

This summer (2016) I played the Monsignor in *Guess Who's Coming to Dinner*. In 1967, the White, liberal newspaper editor's daughter brings home a world-famous Black doctor and says, "We're going to be married."

Her father's head starts swimming with traditional, fearful concerns. The doctor's parents arrive for dinner and *his* father is ready to disown him. The wives' hearts side with their kids and change takes place—art imitating life, except that cultural traditions of life don't change in one day.

Part Three

I just want to be happy, healthy, have peace of mind

Instead of dissecting each of these terms, I'm going to group them under the umbrella term **Well-Being**. I do this partly because the terms are so personal and partly because **Gallup-Healthways** has been amassing a huge database called the **Well-Being Index** (go to http://www.well-beingindex.com/). I introduced this link to my Wellness majors and prepared a Power Point presentation for anyone interested.

A simple way to introduce it to you is the 'ladder assessment.'

- Please imagine a ladder with steps numbered from zero at the bottom to ten at the top. The top of the ladder represents <u>the best possible life for you</u> and the bottom of the ladder represents <u>the worst possible life for you</u>.
- On which step of the ladder would you say you personally feel you stand at this time?
- Please write <u>that</u> number down.

From hundreds of thousands of phone call interviews throughout the U.S. that include other assessment questions, here is one of the results tables that is of particular interest to employers:

7+ = thriving; 4-7= Struggling; <4= Suffering
- Index tabulates Life Evaluation (optimism), Emotional Health, Physical Health, Healthy Behavior, Work Environment, and Basic Access (to healthcare).
- 7+ = 20% lower health insurance claims costs
- <4 = 50% higher health insurance claims costs

See how the next four chapters might help you move to a higher rung on the ladder.

Residents of the Top 10 Well-being Cities in America

1. Learn new and interesting things each day.
2. Have very low rates of clinical depression.
3. Have supervisors at work that treat them like partners, not bosses.
4. Have a lot of energy each day.
5. Have low rates of chronic conditions such as high blood pressure, high cholesterol and diabetes.
6. Have low rates of obesity.
7. Have very few smokers.
8. Find it easy to get clean and safe water.
9. Have safe places to exercise.
10. Have enough money to buy food at all times.
11. Visit the dentist each year.
12. **www.well-beingindex.com**

9.

Your Mind is like a House

Your mind is like a house.

Guests — Promote life and health.

Intruders — Rob us of life and health.

Can you tell a guest from an intruder?

Copyright © 2015 Value Life Associates

Who Rules Your House?

This analogy is intended to help separate <u>you</u> from the constant stream of thoughts flowing through your mind and to build a healthy discernment filter to identify and sort them out. <u>You</u> are **not** your thoughts. <u>You</u> are an individual that can become aware of your thought patterns and take a more active, intentional, decision-making role as to what thoughts are allowed to sit in *your driver's seat*.

Can you tell a guest from an intruder? **Guest thoughts** promote your life and health. **Intruding thoughts** rob you of your life and health, your peace of mind, your joy, and your love. It's that simple. Unwanted thoughts are like unwanted free-loaders living in your house.

How did they get into your mind? When did they come in? Where did they come from? No one was born thinking in English or in your native language, but now that thoughts are dwelling in your mind, what are you going to do about them?

As long as those **intruding thoughts** are in charge, you cannot enjoy the privacy of your own home (they are always bossing you around, telling you what to feel or do). You can't enjoy the peace and quiet (they are always yapping, nagging, whining, and complaining). Do you find it hard to invite in the **guests** (thoughts you really like) that you **want** to spend time with?

You may have thought that you were the house and all its contents. I am suggesting a mind is a house and YOUR mind is YOUR house that you **CAN take charge of!**

You can begin by picking a thought you don't like and asking it a few questions. Let's say it's an *"I can't do it"* thought. *"What benefit do you offer me?" "Have you ever made me happy?" "Who passed you on to me?"* If you ask it, "Why can't I do it?" it will tag-team a series of other intruding thoughts that barged into your house when you were much younger: *"You're dumb." "You're ugly." "You're a wimp." "Mommy won't like it." "You're a chicken."* These are all part of a cobweb of **bully** thoughts passed on to you years ago, but have remained in your subconscious waiting for an occasion to gang up on you. You can learn to disagree with them and substitute the truth for these lies.

Some *apparent* intruders are actually part of an **Early Warning System** trying to alert you to a deeper problem or conflict. Inviting them 'for tea' and a conversation might reveal that your first reading of the thought was a misjudgment. This is not a new idea. Listen to Rumi from 800 years ago:

The Guest House

This being human is a guest house.
Every morning a new arrival.
A joy, a depression, a meanness,
some momentary awareness comes
as an unexpected visitor.
Welcome and entertain them all!
Even if they are a crowd of sorrows,
who violently sweep your house
empty of its furniture,
still, treat each guest honorably.
He may be clearing you out
for some new delight.
The dark thought, the shame, the malice,
meet them at the door laughing and invite them in.
Be grateful for whatever comes,
because each has been sent
as a guide from beyond.
— Jellaludin Rumi, translation by Coleman Barks

On the other hand, some thoughts are just *lies, nags, and misunderstandings* you picked up early in life. Make a decision that you are **not** going to let *them* rule your life, your feelings, or your actions. The more they get their way, the stronger they become and the harder it is to stop them.

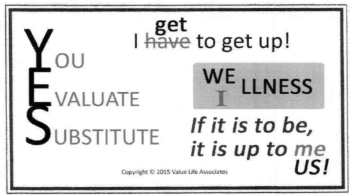

At this time, **you** are the only one that can do the detail work of **evaluating** and changing your mind. Take small, convenient steps by adapting your existing world-view a little here—a little there. Some refer to it as *nudging*. The process usually involves **substituting** one belief for another, one behavior for another, even one habit for another. This card and discussion will make that point clearer.

The **evaluation** process is the same as taking inventory or taking time to discern your own thoughts and feelings. I am presenting a variety of approaches for why and how to go about this challenging and rewarding journey. Here are a few more examples.

Again, in Health class, I would ask a standard question sometime during each semester: *"How many of you had the thought this morning that you **had** to get up?"* Usually, the majority raised their hands. I don't think that's limited to college students. Did you raise your hand?

How many of you know someone, due to an illness or disability, who does not have the choice as to whether or not they will get up? Several raise their hands; many do not. I suggest to those that do not a visit to a hospital or nursing home.

I tell the story of my old friend, Bill, who broke his neck in an altercation on his back porch; it left him a quadriplegic. Bill could only get out of bed when his attendant arrived to clean him up, hoist him up in the lift, and swing him over to his electric wheelchair. Occasionally, I played attendant.

So, what is the truth here? Do <u>you</u> **have** to get up or do <u>you</u> **get** to get up? Do you **have** to get dressed or do you **get** to get dressed? Do you **have** to eat breakfast or do you **get** to eat breakfast?

Go through your day and every time you hear "I **have** to…" go through your mind, **substitute** "I **get** to…" and see what a difference there is in your attitude. We are so privileged to have even the limited choices we do have. We can greatly increase our gratitude by this one **substitution**.

Believe it or not, I was 37 years into teaching health and wellness classes before a student presented me with the simple poster giving the idea that replacing "I" with "WE" can change ILLNESS into WELLNESS. I love it! So often "I" hesitate to ask for help when "I" really need it. I am **substituting** humility for pride whenever I do ask for help.

Around 1991, a new vice president at the university where I was teaching gave a talk entitled, "If it is to be, it is up to me." He was attempting to motivate the student body, but I did not like the singular emphasis. There is an attitude that often goes with *me*-centeredness. I quickly **substituted** "US" for "me" and adopted the phrase as my motto: *If it is to be, it is up to US!* Everything and everyone is in relationship to others, ALL others. That one-word **substitution** is both the truth and it helps my attitude. Powerful stuff.

We can't add to our 24-hour day, but we can become wise in how we **substitute** one thought, one attitude, one behavior for another. There are *those* now practicing the art of changing *their* past and, consequently, the past of others. This practice involves the ability to understand, forgive, and *see* the results unfold in your life.

In Chapter 5, I state, "we can't change the past." It's said in the context of a person who has committed suicide. True, we cannot bring them back to life; but even in that traumatic circumstance, we can learn to go back into our memory banks and substitute more compassion for that person and all who attempt suicide. Great healing can result.

We don't know the intimate internal details of anyone else in the world. We can hear their filtered confessions, read their 'tell-all' autobiographies, hear their braggadocios 'locker room' talk, and be privy to any other sort of revelation without having a clear picture of anyone's full story. You and I don't even have a completely clear picture of the complex influences that created our own bodies, minds, emotions, and relationships.

We need Mercy to forgive ourselves and others—whatever actions have been committed. Forgive the **Self** that was programmed with other's beliefs and was never taught how to separate the **Self** from those beliefs and connected emotions.

What is Discernment?

Discernment, as applied in this context, refers to that ability to distinguish between thoughts that promote <u>health</u> and thoughts that promote <u>illness</u>. To discern means *"to see, to understand, to identify as separate and distinct, to discriminate, to detect. It is a power to see what is not evident to the average mind; emphasizes accuracy, as in reading character, motives, etc."—Webster's Dictionary*

You can start by being skeptical of every thought that goes through your mind. They were all planted by someone else or are coming to you now from this book and, possibly, the Universal Mind. Examine every idea or belief with a magnifying glass. This applies to political, religious and societal beliefs as well as what you believe about yourself.

We all start off unskilled in being a detective looking in our own *house* for clues as to why we're not happy, healthy, or able to love ourselves and others. As with any skill, it takes practice to make progress. The more you evolve your discernment and make life-promoting choices, the happier, healthier, more secure, more peaceful and loving you will become.

As your discernment skill grows, you will feel more trust with the lines of thought you've already examined and it becomes easier to notice the difference between a real intruder's voice and a friend's voice. Your skill will also help you in listening to other voices you encounter through any medium.

This process is not just getting rid of beliefs and ideas, it is the

substitution of new beliefs to replace the old ones. We want to have the truth to answer back to the lie if it comes back around to tempt us. The Bible also refers to the mind as *a house* and to thoughts as *spirits* one has discerned as healthy (clean) or unhealthy (unclean) and starved out (cast out):

> When the unclean spirit is gone out of a man, he walks through dry places, seeking rest, and finds none. Then he says, I will return into my **house** from whence I came out; and when he is come, he finds it empty, swept, and garnished. Then he goes, and takes with himself seven other spirits more wicked than himself, and they enter in and dwell there: and the last state of that man is worse than the first. Even so shall it be also unto this wicked generation. Mat.12:43-45 KJV

This highlights that practice of **substitution**. Just saying, "NO" is not enough. In the place where the intruder stood, a guest (clean spirit/thought) that promotes life and health must stand strongly.

> *"I will not condemn any individual*
> *—including myself.*
> *I believe everyone*
> *is doing the best they can,*
> *every moment,*
> *with the tools they have to work with."* DD

Have you ever wondered about that statement Jesus made while he was on the cross? *"Father, forgive them; for they know not what they do."* (Luke 23:34) Who didn't know what they were doing? Do you know what you are doing? My theory says, they were acting out of a set of unexamined beliefs they had grown up with and Jesus knew it. They did not know they were just *meme*-directed *robots*. That's what we are until we take the time and effort to examine our beliefs.

Discernment Notebook

You will find it helpful to start a Discernment Notebook or journal. The concept is similar to that of a diary. Instead of "Dear Diary" it is "Dear Discernment." Here, you can keep track of when you catch yourself going through the motions of doing things 'you' don't want to do and what keeps you from doing the things you **do** want to do. You can dig into it as deeply as you desire for the **why**.

You can only be conscious of one thought at a time. To capture a thought and learn a pattern of thoughts, you must keep notes like a doctor or a detective. Use your journal to write down the thought patterns and feelings that rip you off as well as your inspirations and revelations.

Throughout life, you can add areas of investigation. You'll be looking for how one reaction leads to another, which leads to another in you and others, until you are caught in a whole *cobweb* of thoughts, emotions, and behaviors. As you discern the *cobwebs*, you can begin to loosen their connections.

Simultaneously, you will be exploring ways to strengthen your own **network** of healthy, life-promoting thoughts, friends, feelings, and behaviors.

This is the most difficult job you will ever accept. The results are clear: chronic confusion can lead to injury, illness, and premature death. Your honest discernment can lead to a healthy life full of happiness, peace, assurance and love. The choices become yours.

Clarification: A notebook alone is not magic. You will also need the help of others who are further along in the process than you are. They know what you are going through and can give you a hand to grab hold of as you climb. You can't do it alone!

After a thorough interior make-over, you will notice that the world outside looks a lot different, too. Enjoy all your new guests and your new view!

Words We Need to Stop Intruders

This chart on the following pages gives you a **Guest List** (We Need) and an **Intruder List** (To Stop). It supplements your own lists of what you want and don't want going on in your mind and your actions.

Use the chart by starting with "**We Need**" followed by a word in the left column (e.g. Appreciation). Continue reading in the middle column "...to be grateful for the life we've been given and the health we can have." Go back to "**We Need** ... **Appreciation** ... **To Stop** ... taking life or health for granted as if someone owed it to us."

Words	We Need	To Stop
Appreciation	... to be grateful for the life we've been given and the health we have.	... taking life or health for granted as if someone owed it to us.
Assurance	... to feel secure in our choices and abilities to promote life.	... doubting that our choices and abilities can promote life.
Boldness	... to stand firm in chosing what's good for us and others.	... being drawn away by tricky, aggressive, snake-oil salesmen.
Commonsense	... to listen to our bodies and follow our intuition.	... over-riding hunches when they are given to us.
Compassion	... to feel deeply for our own and/or another's plight.	... thinking what we or they 'should' or 'shouldn't' do.
Contentment	... to feel a peaceful sense of gratitude for where we are right now.	... comparing our situation to what we 'could' be doing.
Courage	... to risk being alone in our stand for what is right.	... the inner voices that tell us it is too hard.
Courtesy	... to treat others with respect.	... thinking we are better than others.
Dedication	... to commit to a pledge, show up, and stay on the job until it's done.	... thinking our commitments are not important to us or others.
Discernment	... to evaluate and filter the messages we receive & send.	... being an open field and open microphone for anybody's words.
Enthusiasm	... to meet life with a twinkle in our eyes and an eagerness to do our best.	... grumpy complaining thoughts, and feelings of boredom.
Faith	... to hold on to beliefs that pass our scrutiny of skepticism and deep questions.	... constantly second-guessing agreements we have made after carefully weighing the options.
Friendliness	... to treat others as we would want them to treat us.	... treating or ignoring others as if they don't deserve our respect.
Gentleness	... to sooth the aches and pains of living in all its fragility.	... irritating and injuring ourselves or those we meet everyday.
Gratitude	... for all beings and events since the beginning that have brought us to this moment.	... our self-important impression that the world somehow revolves around us.
Happiness	... to enjoy life and help our immune system stay strong.	... complaining about and criticizing every little thing.
Health	... to constantly self-renew our bodies, minds, and spirit.	... living with too much tension or too much sitting still.

I Am NOT My Thoughts!

Words	We Need	To Stop
Honesty	... to face the fact that we are not our thoughts.	... believing the self-right and self-blame chatter our minds repeat.
Hope	... to create an image of the possible and move toward it.	... doubting our capacity to co-create a better future.
Humility	... to see our interdependence with all that exists.	... thinking we do anything without the services of others.
Joy	... to feel a contagious happiness with life.	... being a sour-puss, mule-face, stick-in-the-mud.
Judgment	... to make sound decisions after weighing all sides.	... making reflex decisions out of fear, habit or sense of superiority.
Kindness	... to treat others with the same tenderness we desire.	... injuring others with violence, whether physical or emotional.
Knowledge	... to build a sound body of harmonious beliefs.	... behaving out of ignorance.
Longsuffering	... to pause and remember that maturing is a process.	... making snap judgments and demanding unreasonable growth.
Love	... to believe in the worth of each being and authentically live our lives accordingly.	... believing that some beings don't deserve our respect, kindness, and understanding.
Maturity	... to value life, cooperation, equality, playfulness, the earth, and interdependence.	... holding on to adolescent values of control, violence, patriarchy, fear, separation, and domination.
Mercy	... to forgive ourselves and others, whatever actions have been committed.	... condemning ourselves and others by confusing the individual with its actions.
Moderation	... to stay within our dynamic balance of "Just Right."	... yielding to TOO MUCH or TOO LITTLE in anything.
Obedience	... to follow a code of ethics based on love.	... believing obligations to other's ideas override our code of love.
Patience	... to do our part in the growth process and let nature do hers.	... believing thoughts that want to push the process too fast.
Peace	... to calm both the inner and outer worlds we live in.	... believing the pushy, demanding ideas that shout at us.
Silence	... to listen to the leadings of the Universe, our muse, *God.*	... the noisy distractions inside our minds and all around us.
Understanding	... to see that everything and everyone operates within a broader context.	... assuming we know the meaning of something simply based on what we think happened to us.
Wisdom	... to see both the intended & unintended consequences of our possible plans of action.	... acting for personal or ideological gain without consideration of the Golden Rule.

Think of the vertical line between the **"We Need"** column and the **"To Stop"** column as your **Discernment** line that separates your *guests* from your *intruders*, your flowers from your weeds.

Set up your own plan for repeating the words and phrases often until they become a part of your working body of knowledge. Certainly feel free to add to the chart.

Our thoughts are not us. We are individuals that have thoughts in the language we've been taught. Our thoughts may trigger feelings. Some feelings are good, like joy and love; some don't feel so good, like pain, fear, and hatred. Some thoughts and feelings rob us of our health, our hope, and even life itself. Other thoughts help us through the hardest times and make us soar!

STRESS IS TOO MUCH !

TOO MUCH TENSION AND IT SNAPS –

TOO MUCH DEMAND AND IT STOPS –

TOO MUCH SITTING STILL AND IT DIES –

'IT' IS YOUR { BODY
MIND
EMOTIONS
RELATIONSHIPS
SPIRIT

HEALTH IS JUST RIGHT !

THE PROCESS OF GROWTH

HAS LIMITS FOR STABILITY.

FIND YOURS; USE MODERATION,

COMMONSENSE, AND ENJOY

FITNESS FOR LIFE !

Swimming Hole #9

Some say **discernment** is a gift only a few have, as if it was some kind of absolute truth. It does seem as though some people start out with a more discerning ear, eye, touch, taste, or sense of smell. We also know of some people who lacked or lost certain sensory and/or motor functions that have compensated for it through dedicated effort.

The online dictionary definition of **discernment** includes "*perception in the absence of judgment with a view to obtaining spiritual direction and understanding.*" I believe this kind of discernment only comes as a result of dedicated effort to separate the individual **Self** from its thoughts and actions.

"*Perception in the absence of judgment*" means to me that there is recognition without condemnation, that the discerner sees and hears with love. There is a separation made between the soul and the words, feelings, and actions they are presenting.

What passes for **discernment** is too often just the biased judgments of the teacher who rigidly points out what is socially or religiously acceptable and unacceptable, boxing in their listeners by defining the parameters of obedience and disobedience. This does not meet up with "*perception in the absence of judgment.*"

What is your **discernment** filter? How did you come to see things that way? Is it non-judgmental?

Humor from the Classroom

10.

Stress is Too Much!

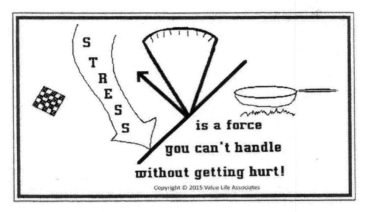

Have you ever accidently picked up a hot iron skillet without using a hotpad? It hurt, didn't it? That scenario is my analogy for stress, *"a force you can't handle without getting hurt!"* Does a hot skillet always hurt you? Not if you use the hotpad. Nothing, in and of itself, is stressful; it's all in how you **handle** it.

To open my health class one day each semester, I'd say, *"Write down the first three words that come to mind when you hear the word STRESS."* [It may be a little late for you readers to do this exercise, but give it a try.] I then asked them to call out their words and I'd write them on the chalkboard. Here are some common examples:

pressure	headaches	homework	bills
girls/boys	relationships	school	tests
children	teachers	police	sex

I then instruct them to only raise their hand once as I go through these three options: *"Stress is only good." "Stress is only bad." "Stress is both good and bad."* Which option gets nearly all their hands in the air? Yep! The last one; the Selye answer. Who is Selye? I'll introduce him in a few pages. Of note here is that his **memes** of *good* and bad stress got embedded in our cultural discourse.

Next, I ask, *"Which of the words on the board is 'good'?"* They quickly realize they were thinking of 'bad' moments related to their words. When they commonly argued, *"But Stress motivates me,"* I'd pick up a long stick I had leaned up against the wall and hold it in a threatening pose. *"Okay, get up or I'll."* They would laugh and get the point.

External threats may temporarily motivate, but the body/mind resists. Boot Camp often includes external threats to the 'green' soldiers so they will be ready to take orders that may end up being against their moral upbringing. *"Makes a man out of him."* I disagree with the tactics and the results.

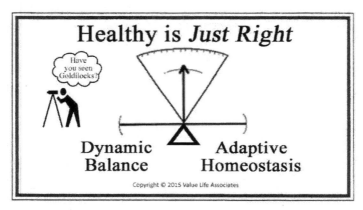

In my Health classes, I used the Goldilocks example for Health and Stress. ***Healthy is Just Right***. Each individual has their *Just Right* for so many things: sleep, food, work, play, touch, temperature, music, etc. It is a range rather than a point on a scale. The range can narrow or widen due to many factors.

Stress is too much. Our body's cells are constantly responding to their environment to maintain our health—an adaptive dynamic balance (homeostasis). Cells can get sabotaged by external and internal forces—including thoughts—that act as ***forces they can't handle without getting hurt***. To get our Health back may require treatment, education, and/or a renewed resolve.

I'm focusing on new **thoughts** and accumulated memories that can be triggered for better or worse. These memories include our **beliefs** that dictate how we perceive the world. If we believe snakes are dangerous, we will perceive them as a threat. Are you afraid of snakes, the dark, rejection, or failure?

Most fears are based on **beliefs** that were established early. Are they worth hanging on to? This is where it gets sticky. We've always thought these fears were protecting us from danger when, in fact, they made us robots to the objects of our fear. Let's take another true story from my classroom experiences: *The Snake Story*.

I am not particularly fond of snakes. When one of my students offered to bring his pet Boa to class to help students with their fear of snakes, I hesitantly said, *"Okay."*

Hoss was about eight feet long with a seven-inch diameter at his mid-section. The student brought him to class in a gunny sack and stretched him out on the eight-foot long lab table in the front of the room. Students were encouraged to come up and touch Hoss, but no one did. The owner said he could drape Hoss over my shoulder and I could walk up and down the two aisles to get him closer to the students. I felt obligated to role model how safe it was (unafraid I was), but I wasn't really happy about it.

Hoss got comfortable with his tail section anchored around my right leg. Finally, he rested his head close to my right shoulder. I did the *runway* walk in the two aisles and the owner put him back in the gunny sack. Whew! That went on for five semesters including one *most interesting* summer session.

That time we were in a classroom that had moveable wooden desks, amphitheater fashion, and about fifty students enrolled. The owner came in with Hoss in the gunny sack, put him behind my desk in the front, and said he'd be right back. I went on with class and, shortly, some students in the front started getting up and moving toward the back. One black male international student actually ran to the back of the room. Hoss had escaped the bag.

What's a teacher to do? *I stepped back and watched.* After a couple of minutes, a white female from the middle of the room came down to Hoss, picked him up, stuffed him back in the bag, and secured the ties. I saw this as a prime teaching moment.

"Why did you run?" "In my village in Nigeria, my parents taught us children, 'Snake? Run! Snake? Run!' It was because we had so many different poisonous snakes close to our village." He was still following those instructions. The young woman said, "I live on a farm. I've pulled lots of black snakes out of our chicken coop."

It challenged the stereotypes so many of us grew up with.

Hoss's final visit the next Spring was business as usual until I concluded my walk. At that moment, Hoss (Kaa) did the **_Jungle Book_** stare: his head came up and we were nearly nose to nose. I only knew not to make any quick movements. As the sweat rolled down my sides due to the perceived threat, I quietly called for the owner to remove Hoss.

That was his last ride on my shoulder. About a month later, a student brought me a clipping from the _Kansas City Star_. "7th Grade Science teacher killed by Boa in front of students." The classroom **Boa** had wrapped around him and **constricted**. I saw the foolish risk I had been taking. Lesson learned.

Let's examine the Physiology of Stress.

Fall 1980. My friend Ted Dreisinger was hired to run a hospital-based Wellness program we named **_Fitness for Life_**. Not yet having a job, I had volunteered to tag along and help. One day the hospital administrator asked me, _"Dalton, isn't there something you can do to get paid? Can you teach stress management classes?"_ I had never had a class in stress management, but this brand new PhD Health Educator of course said, _"Yes."_

I quickly reviewed the literature and saw there were two _camps_: those that believed stress was bad for your health and those that followed Dr. Hans Selye who had added _eustress_ (good stress) to the public lexicon in 1956 with his book, **_The Stress of Life_**. I had not heard of 'good' stress in any of my college courses and my personal take on stress said it was something to reduce or avoid.

The earliest definition I came across that applied to health and illness was from the 1949 **Conference on Life and Stress and Heart Disease**. They defined stress as "**a force** _that induces distress or strain upon both the emotional and physical make-up._" That was very close to the definition I found in my **_Webster's American Heritage Dictionary_** in 1980: _"a force that tends to deform a body and act as a mentally or emotionally disruptive influence."_

I also found _"STRESS"_ by Dr. Selye in the **_THE ROTARIAN Magazine_** (March 1978). He began by saying,

> "Nobody can escape stress because to eliminate it completely would mean to destroy life itself! ...The technical definition of stress implies the body's response to *any* demand. Stress is essential in our day-to-day living. It is the spice of life ...Distress, of course, is the opposite of eustress."

I was shocked by his last paragraph several pages later:

> "Wouldn't it be better if we could find a way to prevent the stress of life, rather than simply means to help us fight a hostile world? I believe that this should be our highest priority in formulating the policies of governments to meet the stresses of modern civilization, and in devising our personal philosophies of life."

I wondered if I was the only one who read all the way to the end? Nearly every textbook, article and workshop on stress would parrot Dr. Selye's first page ideas of *good stress* and *bad stress* never mentioning his **highest priority** of **preventing the stress of life**. I titled my classes, *Health Resists Stress*. My highest priority was preventing the stress of life. It still is.

Selye had switched the definition of stress in 1956 from **a force** acting on the mind and body to "the body's **response** to *any* demand." That new definition meant that every response, even breathing, was stressful. For me, Selye's definition would rob me of the term *health* and I was a Health Educator! It seemed his goal wasn't health, but optimum levels of stress.

You'll get to decide whose definition of stress you buy into, but I'd say, at a gut level, you believe stress is bad for you. So, "Wouldn't it be better if we could find a way to prevent the stress of life, rather than simply means to help us fight a hostile world?"

Selye's research did provide us with the **General Adaptation Syndrome**, three stages labeled Alarm, Action and Fatigue for an animal's common physiologic response to perceived danger. I created this simple chart to express it. This is the "threat to control" pathway pictured in the '**Physiology of Emotional Stress**' chart.

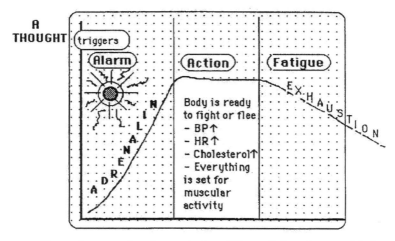

Since then, we've learned that "freeze" has been added to Walter B. Cannon's phrase, "fight or flight," because so many people respond that way to a perceived threat.

I created the following chart of **Healthy Substitutes** for the Alarm, Action, and Fatigue stages of the G.A.S. Each of these is tried and true *"to prevent the stress of life."* The chart was created in the middle 1980s and I'm glad to say it has stood the test of time.

Healthy Substitutes

Discernment	Exercise	Relaxation
- Learn to catch the thoughts that lead to the Adrenalin reaction and defuse their effects on your system. - Learn why you feel threatened, why you are so defensive, why you can't seem to handle criticism. - Learn what you are really afraid of!!!	- Engage in some regular heart pumping exercise 3-5 times each week. - Do NOT exercise in a competitive manner. This is for your health & can be fun!! - Try to break a light sweat without huffing & puffing.	- Build regular relaxation periods into your daily schedule. - Feel the benefits of deep breathing, progressive muscle relaxation, focusing, vacation breaks, and message. - Laughing, playing games, hobbies, etc. can be great!

Another 'new' finding had to do with reduced bloodflow to the pre-frontal cortex during this General Adaptation Syndrome

(G.A.S.). If you truly perceive you are in imminent danger, bloodflow to the pre-frontal cortex (the seat of moral judgment) is reduced in favor of the limbic system (pre-programmed reactions). You won't be thinking straight.

If you perceive a threat, ASAP take some 'time-out' to calm down. Long-term, "**catch the thoughts** that lead to the Adrenalin reaction and <u>defuse</u> their effects on your system." To <u>defuse</u> means to replace the fuse (the thought/belief) that triggers the cascading reaction with an alternate viewpoint. As you saw in Chapter 9, I focus on **Substitution** as the primary tool for this job.

Other research took me to an article which described two kinds of stress: threat to control (alarm followed by fight or flight) and loss of control (depression from helpless/hopeless beliefs). These are the adrenalin and cortisol pathways. Both are considered unhealthy when chronic and both start with a perceived stimulus (a thought) that triggers coping patterns both genetic and learned.

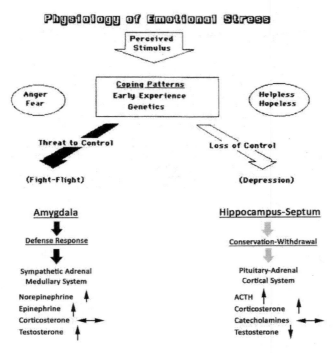

The Physiologic Response to Emotional Stress

Rather than a social stimulus acting directly on you to produce a physical reaction, it is now clear that **your perception of a situation**, filtered through your own self-image and value system, brings about one or more physiologic responses. In other words, **"It's not so much what happens to you, but how you take it."** When a situation is perceived as a threat or a challenge, anxiety is aroused. When a situation is seen as important to you personally, but you feel unable to control the outcome (i.e. helpless, hopeless), depression is triggered.

The **perceived** threat or challenge causes the pituitary gland in the brain to activate the sympathetic and adrenal medullary responses. Primarily, in this alarm response, **adrenalin** alerts the body in such a way as to prepare the large muscle groups to work most effectively. This means more blood to those muscles and less to the gut and extremities. [And now we know this includes less blood the pre-frontal cortex of the brain].

- Heartrate and blood pressure go up
- Respirations increase
- Pupils dilate
- Hearing becomes more acute
- Blood cholesterol levels elevate
- More blood sugar is available for energy
- [And now we know the ability to make moral judgments is reduced]

This is the body's way of giving you every opportunity to reflexively protect your life whenever you perceive you are threatened. Disease will result when these perceptions are chronic without the follow-through of vigorous activity.

The article continues on the next page. This second response was seldom included in common stress presentations, possibly because Dr. Selye did not seem to include it. In 1989, I read, *Is It Worth Dying For?* by Dr. Robert S. Eliot and Dennis L. Breo. There, this second response was referred to as "The Long-term Vigilance Reaction." You will recognize the emotions triggered by the perceptions of being helpless and/or hopeless to change a circumstance you deem important to you or another.

The **helpless, hopeless feeling**, along with **lack of self-worth**, triggers the release of **ACTH** which activates other body chemicals and leads to:

- **Mental depression**
- **Decreased sex drive**
- **Increased stomach acidity**
- **Hypertension**
- **Slowed heart rate**
- **Decreased ability to resist disease**

On the other hand, when you feel socially **accepted** and/or have a high sense of **self-worth**, the physiologic response is reversed. You

- **Are mentally active,**
- **Have normal sex drives,**
- **Have decreased stomach acidity,**
- **Have normal heartrate and blood pressure,**
- **Are better able to resist disease.**

Throughout this book, the focus has been on thoughts and their role in promoting our health or our illness. This more detailed presentation of the physiologic response to emotional stress is aimed at the exact same point, the power of our perceptions, which are the outcomes of our beliefs (paradigms). For fans of **_The Shack_** by Wm. Paul Young, you may recognize this quote:

Paradigms power perception
and perceptions power emotions.
Most emotions are responses to perception -
what you think is true about a given situation.
If your perception is false,
then your emotional response to it will be false too.
So check your perceptions,
and beyond that
check the truthfulness of your paradigms -
what you believe.
Just because you believe something firmly
doesn't make it true.
Be willing to reexamine what you believe.

Swimming Hole #10

The Goal

Stress goes back to a thought you've been taught
that you cannot yet control:
a fear, a doubt, an anger, a hurt,
that stabs into your soul.
I'm right. I'm wrong. I'm so confused,
I don't even know who I am.
I want to do right, but there's so much to fight,
and nobody else gives a damn.

There will come a day when a stranger will say,
"I know who you are; why you're here.
Someone told me, when I couldn't see,
And things began to get clear.
But I'll tell you right now,
you'll never know how
if you don't want to shoulder this task.
The answers are there,
but you'll never know where
until you begin to ask.

Discernment's the key for you and for me,
an abundance of fruit is our goal.
But right now there's a mess because of this stress
that stabs into your soul.
So go after the weeds and plant in new seeds
and cultivate a good crop.
Work it each day (there's no other way)
and your benefits won't ever stop."

© R.B. Dalton 1988

11.

Can you find your Self?

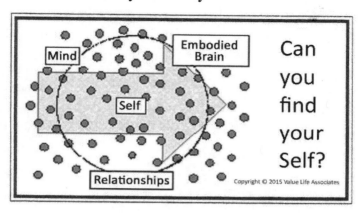

Stages of Self-Awareness

For most of us, self-awareness first occurred sometime between ages one and three. Before that could happen, a lot had to transpire. We *could* go all the way back to *God* or the *Big Bang*; but let's start with a sperm bumping into an egg in a warm, dark Fallopian tube.

The **Embodied Brain** was introduced to me by Dr. Bruce Lipton in his book, ***The Biology of Belief.*** From the moment a sperm has an intimate **relationship** with an egg, all the baby's cell membranes are constantly responding to their environment (epigenetics). As cells specialize into three layers (ectoderm, mesoderm, and endoderm), the skull brain and neural connections develop from the same outer layer as our skin.

Beyond that, let's acknowledge the complexities in using the term "brain." In the **"Skull Brain"** we have the brainstem, cerebellum, limbic system, and cerebrum (cerebral cortex with its special pre-frontal cortex). Each has its evolutionary history and interrelated complexities. It's now recognized that we also have a **"Heart Brain"** (originating in the mesoderm) and a **"Gut Brain"** (originating in the endoderm), each with their unique and interrelated complexities. So 'brain' is not only in the skull, it's

105

embodied—connected to and embedded in the entire body.

Relationships. *Everything is in relationship to everything else*; this seems to be **one of those eternal truths**. Nothing exists alone or outside of relationships. Some relationships are obvious and easily defined (e.g. family, friends, society, nature), but most of our relationships go unnoticed (e.g. our cells that live, work and die in relationship to each other to keep us alive and healthy; all the people it takes to get food onto our plates; all the invisible, silent, energetic relationships with all the other energies in this living Universe).

Mind is defined by a quote from Dr. Dan Siegel, a keynote speaker I heard at a **National Wellness Conference**:

> "**MIND** is an Emergent,
> Self-organizing
> Process
> that arises from the interactions
> of the elements of a system—
> i.e. from the flow of energy
> within embodied neural activity
> and relational communication."

As the multiple **elements** (the small circles on the card) of the developing bio-social **systems interact**, the **mind** (psycho) **E**merges and begins its **S**elf-organizing **P**rocess which continues until energy/spirit (the big arrow) no longer flows through the complete bio-psycho-social-spiritual system.

Once an undefined quantity and/or quality of **interactions** have occurred with those around the child—who related to the child as a unique person with a name, a nickname, and/or various descriptive adjectives—an **"A-ha" moment occurs in the child.** Speculating that my granddaughter was experiencing *that* moment as she took an extended look at herself in a mirror around the age of two, I wondered if she was thinking, "*I am the one they have been talking about*." **Self** is born in the pre-frontal cortex.

Certainly, there had been oodles of data collection prior to *that*. The emerging mind was networking stimulus-response patterns, mapping the body in space, and sharpening skills. Let me ask some questions usually considered philosophical or religious.

The way I am using **Self** is equal to the way most religions would refer to **Soul**. **Self/Soul** is the individual: observant when aware and decisive when given a choice. It can deepen in its awareness or continue to see only through the unexamined beliefs of others.

> What can we say of **Self** while that data collection and wiring was going on? Did **Self** exist before **Self**-awareness? Where? Is the **Self** (Soul) truly immortal – endlessly coming from and going to another time or dimension? Has the **Self** lived in another form? Who could be the authority on answering these questions?

Toltec wisdom, as passed on to us in *The Fifth Agreement* by don Miguel Ruiz and his son don Jose Ruiz, refers to this first stage of awareness as *The Dream of the First Attention* or being the "Victim." The **Self**, with its Mind, Embodied Brain, and Relationships, is subject to all the forces with which it interacts. It gets loaded with labels and biased **beliefs**.

This conditioned awareness is captured in a description by **Dr. Gabor Mate** in **Yes! Magazine** (Nov. 2015):

> "During our dependent and vulnerable childhoods, we develop the psychological, behavioral, and emotional composite that later we **mistake** for ourselves. This composite, which we call the personality, often **masks** a real person with real needs and desires. The **personality** is not a fault – in stressed environments it **evolves primarily as a defense**, a defense that can turn saboteur." [my emphasis]

Common Defense Mechanisms

Denial	Blocking	Intellectualization
Projection	Acting Out	Displacement
Isolation	Introjection	Somatization
Regression	Undoing	Rationalization
Repression	Splitting	Passive-Aggressive
Dissociation	Lying	Reaction Formation

Psychology tells us that a healthy development into adulthood **sheds those defense mechanisms**. Shedding the old 'skin' requires another revelation triggering the Toltec "Warrior" stage, *The Dream of the Second Attention*. That move will depend a great deal on messages one **hears** from their internal and external teachers. *Those that have ears to **hear**, let them **hear**.*

Self will begin to see that all its labels, all its **beliefs**, came directly or indirectly from other people and it is time to be skeptical of it all—to question what has already been planted in the Mind and to listen to what others are saying with a new *ear*.

This "Warrior" stage of **Self**-examination can be likened to the Biblical battle of *Armageddon* or *"The Hero's Journey."* It is difficult and takes much humility, courage, and dedication. There are many tools and spiritual *weapons* offered by teachers around the world.

> **The Five Agreements:**
> 1) Be impeccable with your word;
> 2) Don't take anything personally;
> 3) Don't make assumptions;
> 4) Always do your best; and
> 5) Be skeptical, but learn to listen.

Those that take the journey seriously, as a discipline, arrive at the "Master" stage. Here, in *The Dream of the Third Attention*, you have won this personal war; you are at peace, and full of love.

As a "Master," you're aware that you (the **Self**) are not your body, thoughts or spirit. Your skill in observing with your physical and spiritual senses has sharpened and your decisions reflect a depth of wisdom that sees both intended and unintended consequences.

In the fourth Toltec stage, you are a **Self**-Transcendent, deep "Seer" and *Messenger of the Great Mystery*. You *see* those **Souls** that are struggling in the "Victim" stage; "Warriors" seeking to redefine their own **beliefs** and behaviors; and "Masters" as they become **Self**-Actualized. Your presence can be joyful, sober, firm, or full of compassion. You respect all beings. You behave as a Loving, Playful Servant—as a *Social Artist* who lives the words of Diane Ackerman:

> "I swear I will not dishonor my soul with hatred,
> but offer myself humbly as a guardian of nature,
> as a healer of misery, as a messenger of wonder,
> as an architect of peace."

Speaking of *Social Artist*, let me officially introduce one of my mentors, Dr. Jean Houston, the co-creator of **Social Artistry**. I have known Jean and benefitted personally and professionally from her work since meeting her in 2001. Two of the most popular of her thirty-plus books are *The Possible Human* and *A Mythic Life*. I believe our first 'meeting' was mythic and worth sharing.

Around 1981, as a member of our local chapter of the **American Society for Training and Development** (ASTD), I was given a cassette tape of a possible keynote speaker for an upcoming regional conference. Circumstances related to my responsibilities with my church prevented me from listening to the tape and from even going to the conference.

Fast-forward twenty years—2001; my wife and I have left the church and at school I received an announcement of the **National Wellness Institute's** summer conference entitled *2001 Wellness Odyssey*. Jean Houston was listed as one of the keynote speakers.

At home, as I sat at my desk, I reached into the shallow middle drawer and pulled out that never-before-listened-to cassette tape from 1981 with the name Jean Houston written on it. I popped it into my boom box and listened. By the end of the tape I was weeping as deeply as ever in my life and I had slithered to the floor. It was as if I was being embraced by a great knowing; a deep and ancient yearning was being answered and called forth.

Needless to say, I went to the conference, listened to her 'okay' keynote, and participated with several hundred others in her very engaging afternoon workshop. There, among many other things, she introduced us to our *Entelechy*. This is her term for our fulfilled **Self**, the deep **Seer** we were always meant to become and are becoming, our great Friend that draws us toward our fulfillment with a deep love.

I *saw* my *Entelechy*, talked to it, became my *Entelechy* for a short time, and know now it is only a thought away. This is not one's every day experience and I can't expect you to know what I'm talking about unless you, too, have experienced it. I share the story because it must be included in a discussion of **Self**.

One more story from another exercise with Jean at one of her **West Coast Mystery School** weekends in 2002. She had all of a hundred or so participants spread out in a large meeting room with appropriate background music playing. She asked us to see if we noticed our **Self** in the past as she called out "*50 years ago, 100 years ago, 200 years ago…*". This went on and on and on and I was sure this exercise was not 'working' for me. Then she said, "*10,000 years ago.*" Immediately, I was a Kalahari Desert tribal woman nursing my son at my left breast. After a while, I drew him from my breast and held him up face-forward in front of me as I offered him to the future with the dreams of my people. Then, suddenly, I was back in the room.

What happened? Was I hallucinating? Did I shift into a parallel world? Did **Self**, as a ***pod of consciousness***, travel to a different time and space—into a previous incarnation? I believe the latter explanation to be the most plausible. This whole subject of 'incarnation' and 'reincarnation' has threads through most cultures of the world. Much of our quest to "Know thy **Self**" seems connected to these threads. I encourage you to be curious and open to personal leadings on your trip.

I recommend Jean's book *The Wizard of Us* as a companion reader on your journey. I used it as a textbook in one of my Mental/Emotional/Spiritual Wellness classes. You'll be fascinated at how much you'll find in "your own back yard."

As I mentioned earlier, one of her many transformative exercises introduces you to your higher (fulfilled) **Self**, your *Entelechy*. As she describes in *The Wizard of Us*,

> *Entelechy* is a Greek word that means "the fullest realized essence of a thing." For example, a grand oak tree is the entelechy of an acorn.

Here is my modified version of Jean's *Entelechy* exercise. Sometimes it helps to have a friend calmly and lovingly read the instruction box to you. As Jean says, "*Whatever works.*"

Meeting Your Entelechy

> To experience this connection, take a moment now to stand comfortably straight with your weight balanced equally on both feet. Close your eyes. Take three deep breaths through your nose as if you're filling up and emptying a balloon located behind your belly button. With each breath, feel your body relaxing.

Now imagine, standing before you in a body of light, is your entelechy—the Great Friend. You greet each other warmly. Now raise both hands with your palms facing forward as your entelechy does the same. As your palms gently touch, your entelechy begins to beam waves of love into you. You take them in. Wisdom, compassion, kindness, strength—all those things are being poured into you now through this Great Friend. Do this for a few minutes. Receive, receive, receive.

With your physical body, now step forward and turn around in the place where the entelechy was standing, facing the spot you just left. Keep your hands raised and touch the imaginary hands of your local **Self** with your palms. You have now become the entelechy beaming energy, love, power, gratitude, and blessings into your local **Self**. Do this for a few minutes. Tell the local **Self** how much you honor and love it.

With your physical body, step forward and turn around again, returning to the spot where you originally stood, palms out, facing the Great Friend. Once again receive all the good things that the entelechy is offering you. Feel yourself being filled, revitalized and energized.

You may wish to repeat these steps until you feel infused with the light and energy of your Great Friend. When you've finished, thank your entelechy. Know that this higher **Self** loves you and is always available for you.

When you're ready, take a few more deep breaths, return to the room, and open your eyes. How do you feel?

In many mythical stories and fairy tales, the fulfilled **Self** is depicted as a separate character. Dorothy's Entelechy in *The Wizard of Oz*, would be Glinda, the good Witch of the North.

For those of you who share Christian roots with me, a perfected Jesus could be viewed as your Entelechy or fulfilled **Self**. Although many Christian leaders may try to tell you it's impossible, read for yourself this passage attributed to Paul:

And he gave some, apostles; and some, prophets; and some, evangelists; and some, pastors and teachers; For the **perfecting** of the saints, for the work of the ministry, for the **edifying** of the body of Christ: Till we **all** come in the **unity** of the faith, and of the knowledge of the Son of *God*, unto a **perfect** man, unto the measure of the stature of the **fullness** of Christ: That we *henceforth* be no more children, tossed to and fro, and carried about with every wind of doctrine, by the sleight of men, *and* cunning craftiness, whereby they lie in wait to deceive; But speaking the truth in **love**, may grow up into him in all things, which is the head, *even* Christ: From whom the whole body fitly joined together and compacted by that which every joint supplies, according to the effectual working in the measure of every part, makes increase of the body unto the **edifying of itself in love**. (Eph.4:11-16)

111

Each **Soul** acquires access to a unique mixture of healthy and unhealthy qualities as a child. As we later *conceive* the idea that we are not those qualities and learn to feed the healthy ones and starve out the unhealthy ones, we can eventually be *born again*. From there we have the whole growing up and maturing process until we attain "the fullness of Christ" — a Christ depth of awareness with all those qualities of the Spirit uniquely mixed in us to their complete and ripe perfection.

Swimming Hole #11

Speaking of fulfilled **Selves**, entertain this possibility: Earth (Gaia), as a collective being (**Self**), began to 'wake up'—become **Self**- conscious—when human Earthlings saw Earth's image in that first photograph taken in 1969. As the first stage of **Self**-awareness, it will surely and gradually lead all the way to the Possible—Fulfilled—World (**Self**).

This possibility clearly includes human beings as intricately and intimately part of Gaia. We are all part of the awakening. One of Jean's favorite quotes is from Christopher Fry's play, *A Sleep of Prisoners*:

The human heart can go to the lengths of *God*...
Dark and cold we may be, but this
Is no winter now. The frozen misery
Of centuries breaks, cracks, begins to move;
The thunder is the thunder of the floes,
The thaw, the flood, the upstart Spring.
Thank *God* our time is now when wrong
Comes up to face us everywhere,
Never to leave us till we take
The longest stride of soul men ever took.
Affairs are now soul size.
The enterprise is exploration into *God*.
Where are you making for? It takes
So many thousand years to wake...
But will you wake, for pity's sake?

12.

Circumcision of the Heart?

In my **Personal and Community Health** classroom, I would start each class with music, a quote on the TV monitors, and several student posters displayed. One of my favorite quotes was by **Alexander Solzhenitsyn:**

> If only there were evil people somewhere
> committing evil deeds, and it were necessary
> only to separate them from the rest of us
> and destroy them.
> But the line dividing good and evil cuts through
> the heart of every human being.
> And who is willing
> to destroy a piece of his own heart?

I would ask for a show of hands for those who were willing to destroy a piece of their own heart. Rarely would a hand go up.

I then would start a discussion of circumcision—what seemed to most, an unrelated topic. What do you think? How would you relate the two? [I certainly did not relate them before I was part of an in-depth *Bible* study which served as the foundation of my ministerial training.]

In the class discussion, I talked about Abram and Sarai, the promise of a child, Ishmael being born to Hagar, the command for circumcision, and the tradition which continues to this day among Jews, Muslims and Christians. We discussed some of the ways the operation was performed and how it even expanded into female genital mutilation of young girls.

Biblically and culturally the origination of circumcision seems clear. What was the purpose? Does circumcision make one healthier? In the USA, parents challenged the routine circumcision of their sons in the early 1960s. Research was done for several decades. It revealed that the circumcised men have only slightly lower rates of infection than uncircumcised men. It is now an elective surgery requiring consent.

As far as female genital mutilation, there is a huge outcry among women's rights activists around the world calling for the end of this horrific practice that robs the female of physical sexual pleasure. Tradition is very difficult to change.

But did circumcision start for physical health reasons? Was there possibly another purpose? The **Bible** and concordance are available for all to see other places circumcision is mentioned. I put the following verse from Deuteronomy 30:6 on the overhead:

> And the LORD thy God
> will circumcise thine heart,
> and the heart of thy seed,
> to love the LORD thy God
> with all thine heart,
> and with all thy soul,
> that you may live

Very few of my twenty thousand students had ever seen this verse before even though the vast majority were Judeo-Christian-Muslim of some fashion. What could *the LORD thy God* mean by this? How would it be accomplished? It cannot be talking about the blood-pumping heart. It appears to liken the 'heart' to a person's mind and/or emotions. That makes it another analogy.

It is interesting to me that the Hebrew word for **health** was also translated as **salvation**. The two ideas of the card are brought together as one. If anything in your heart prevents you from loving *the LORD thy God* with **all** your heart, it appears you need to search and destroy that piece of your heart so you can have **health**.

Solzhenitsyn says it is *evil* that one might consider cutting away or destroying. The language here seems steeped in religion, but it is a common teaching in many cultures around the world untouched by the Judeo/Christian/Muslim traditions. Let us consider the popular Native American Proverb:

> A Native American grandmother wore a necklace with two wolf heads on it. Her grandson asked, "Why do you have two wolf heads on your necklace?" She said, "I feel as if I have two wolves fighting in my heart. One wolf is the angry, violent, vengeful one. The other wolf is the loving, kind, compassionate one." The grandson asked her, "Which wolf will win the fight in your heart?" She answered, "The one I feed."

Once again, the heart is the site of struggle or division between opposing emotions that stem from one's **beliefs**. If you believe you are right and someone else is wrong, you may find yourself angry. You may want to 'get back' at someone if you believe they have 'wronged' you, your family, or your country. Violence—violence of every kind—is based on this common self-right **belief**.

Two wolves struggling in my heart.

The Angry, Vengeful, Violent Wolf.

The Kind, Loving, Merciful Wolf.

Which one will win? The one I feed.

Value Life Associates

This sets up that deep discernment question: Which one will win? We are simply *victims* and *slaves* until we are able to separate **Self** from the *Wolves*. **I** have thoughts, but **I** am not my thoughts. **I** have

beliefs, but **I** can change any **belief** that **I** (**Self**) choose to change. **I** have emotions, but they are not me. **I** have been a *slave*, but **I** can be released from my *mental slavery*. **I** was ignorant of the power of my pre-programmed **beliefs**, but now, by examining my **beliefs**, feeding the healthy ones, and starving the unhealthy ones, **I** can turn the tables on who is in charge and fulfill my potential.

Here is another story from another culture found in ***The Tao of Physics*** by Fritjof Capra:

> "As the *God* speaks, the realistic background of the war between the two families soon fades away and it becomes clear that the battle of Arjuna is <u>the spiritual battle of human nature</u>, the battle of the warrior in search of enlightenment. Krishna himself advises Arjuna:

> "Kill therefore with the sword of wisdom
> the doubt born of ignorance that lies in thy heart.
> Be one in self-harmony, in Yoga,
> and arise, great warrior, arise."

Hindu Vedas/Upanishads/Mahabharata/Bhagavad Gita

Amazingly, we find another analogy for the heart and a sword used to kill or destroy a part of that heart. In this instance, it is *the sword of wisdom* (also see Eph.6:17) that will cut away *the doubt born of ignorance*. That will take some serious wisdom, honesty and humility to face one's own doubts and admit you have been ignorant or wrong. But only then can you arise in **Self**-harmony—discord and violence gone. Who is willing to be such a *spiritual warrior*?

So much of our lives have involved 'put-downs' that produce self-condemnation. **We were raised to doubt** our ability to be free of sin, free of unskilled behaviors, free of judging ourselves and others, free of guilt and shame, free to explore our full capacities.

Yet the wisdom teachers from around the world have suggested and told us to do exactly that. In Mat.5:48 (KJV) Jesus said, *"Be ye therefore perfect, even as your Father which is in heaven is perfect."* Why tell us to do something impossible? Maybe the wisdom teachers know something we don't yet know.

The apostle Paul is said to have been sent to the Gentiles (the uncircumcised) and we have many of his letters to ponder. Here is one little verse.

> Circumcision is nothing, and uncircumcision is nothing, but the keeping of the commandments of God. (1 Co. 7:19)

It doesn't matter if you've been physically circumcised or not; keep the commandments of God. Which ones? Jesus said, *to live* you must:

> ...love the Lord thy God with all thy heart, and with all thy soul, and with all thy strength, and with all thy mind; and thy neighbor as thyself. (Luke 10:25-28; Mark 12:28-31)

In order to grow our **love** to its fullest capacity, we get to kill the doubt in our hearts, circumcise our hearts, and stop feeding the angry, vengeful, violent wolf in our hearts. It is **not** impossible.

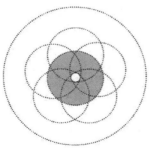

I Am NOT My Thoughts!

Swimming Hole #12

What is the difference between the Ten Commandments of Moses and the Two stated by Jesus? We see a world controlled by fear when Moses got the Tablets of Stone. Break any one of seven of the ten commandments and you'd be stoned to death. Check it out.

Jesus brought a new message that would require followers to go through a paradigm shift in their own minds. Love and fear are not compatible.

Most Christians are not taught that "Thy kingdom come...in earth" applies to the earth of their minds. Most are looking for Jesus to come and set up a physical kingdom even though Jesus said, "Yet a little while and the world seeth me no more." (Joh.14:19) He also said, "Neither shall they say, Lo here! or, lo there! for, behold, the kingdom of *God* is within you." (Luk.17:21)

That kingdom is ruled by love, joy, peace, and mercy. No religious group in the world has a corner on these powerful qualities. Atheist and agnostics can have the same paradigm shift from fear to love, joy, peace, mercy, compassion, patience, and all the rest of the fruits of the Spirit.

It requires replacing one **old belief** that results in fear with a **new belief** that results in love. This is pictured by the cutting away of the foreskin of a man's penis, the organ that delivers the seeds, but the intent is to make the change in our hearts. This book is all about changing your heart (emotions) and mind (beliefs/*memes*).

Let these thoughts swim around a bit. Do you believe it's possible? What could possibly limit you?

Part Four

Keep asking questions
until the answers make sense

The power of asking questions cannot be overstated. When we are not asking questions, is it because we are content in the moment? Contentment is a wonderful quality. It is one of the Words We Need back in Chapter 9. "We need **contentment** to feel a peaceful sense of gratitude for where we are right now. We need **contentment** to stop comparing our situation to what we 'could' be doing. Yet, contentment does not drug our curiosity and interest.

Another possibility is a dull, sleepy condition of the mind where we are resigned to what is and nothing we do is going to change that. One more possibility is the manner in which people have responded to our interest and curiosity expressed by questions. Teachers and/or peers in school may have indicated that our questions were not welcomed or valued.

Sometimes church leaders suppress the asking of questions about the Bible or about *God*. Why would that pattern of behavior be so prevalent in Christianity when Jesus plainly said, "Ask and you'll receive; seek and you'll find; knock and the door will be opened to you?

The next four chapters strongly encourage asking questions until the answers make sense. I certainly ask you enough questions throughout the course of this book. I don't need to know your answers, but I believe you do.

A little humor from the Cave Room.

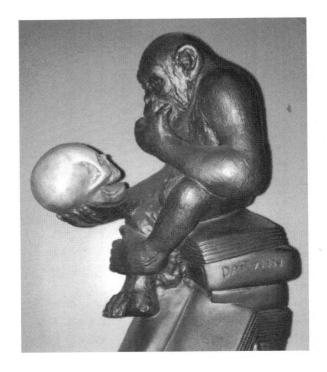

13.

There are Depths to Understanding

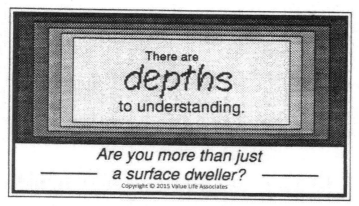

There are
depths
to understanding.

*Are you more than just
a surface dweller?*

Copyright © 2015 Value Life Associates

An educated guess says all of you reading this went to elementary school, secondary school, and probably some or a lot of higher education. That means you clearly know about lesser and deeper depths of understanding many things.

That is indeed one application of the card, but not the only one. "A surface dweller" can refer to the times we take things at face value without question. We all do that. Then there are times we **dig for more understanding by asking questions**; maybe a lot of them. Here are a few examples you may be familiar with.

Thousands of students and teachers had seen the picture in their biology textbook of a Black woman connected to the discovery of HeLa cells, but only one that we know of was stirred to ask questions about the woman. In the Prologue of her best-selling book, ***The Immortal Life of Henrietta Lacks***, Rebecca Skloot shares her first questions. "*Where was she from?*" "*Did she have any children?*" From seeing the photograph (physical/sensory = **L1**), she kept on **digging deeper** for answers about this woman (historical and psychological = **L2**) until she finally got to the bottom of it.

By the time students arrived in my **Personal and Community Health** class as freshmen in college, they seldom asked questions. When they did ask, it was common to hear, "Is that going to be on

121

the test?" Our educational system seems to have conditioned so many of our youth to stop asking questions that could lead to deeper understanding. *That* curiosity expressed out loud was rare in the college classroom. That's a sad outcome of our school system.

At a distant time and place, a multitude of people and a few disciples had heard the teacher tell a parable (mythic/symbolic = **L3**) about a sower sowing seeds into four different kinds of soil (wayside, stony, thorny, good ground). We only have a record of one disciple asking, "What might this parable be?" Jesus said:

> Unto you it is given to know the mysteries of the kingdom of God: but to others in parables; that seeing, they might not see, and hearing they might not understand. (Luk. 8:10)

"Mysteries" refer to a deeper depth of understanding. Why were the disciples the only ones who would get it? Was it pre-determined by the biblical *God* and had nothing to do with their choices or is there another explanation? These disciples had been looking for the prophesied Messiah for a long time. They had heard John the Baptist speak a message of one coming that was more powerful than himself and they believed him. They obviously were seekers with questioning minds.

Since you're reading this book, it appears you also have a questioning mind. What questions are you asking? Are you on a **quest for understanding**? You've asked questions before. Were you told it was wrong to question *God* or that it was impossible to understand the mysteries of the Universe? I know many who had that experience.

Jesus went on to explain the mystery of the parable. **Seeds are words**. The four kinds of soil are four possible conditions of someone's mind when they hear words. Sometimes your mind is in a wayside condition: words 'go in one hear and out the other.' Sometimes you get excited when you hear a new idea, but let go of the idea when others laugh at or criticize it. Sometimes you just get too busy with life to pursue the power of the cool idea you recently heard. And sometimes...

> "... the good ground are they which in an honest and good heart, having heard the word, [and understand it], keep it and bring forth fruit with patience." (Mat.13:23; Luk.8:15)

It seems that Jesus never did **surface level** (L1) talks. He didn't even do **historical/psychological** (L2) talks. His teaching was always **mythic/symbolic** (L3), always in parables (Mat. 8:34 "*without a parable spake he not unto them.*") This is <u>esoteric</u> language ("designed for and understood by the specially initiated alone" - Webster's New Collegiate Dictionary, 1973). As in many disciplines, you need to ask questions of your teacher (you're on a quest) and collect lots of data/experience. You'll start with a rudimentary understanding and the more you apply the lessons, the deeper your understanding becomes.

Another mystery revealed in the seed sower parable is "*You are not your thoughts.*" Did you catch that? The seed sower is anyone playing the *male role* in *social intercourse*. The message (words or *memes*) is not the messenger and when you receive them (the words or *memes*) they do not become you. They get sown into your ground (*heart* or mind) and may or may not become a part of your *body of knowledge*. Did the disciples instantly understand that? No.

Just hearing someone tell you what a word or phrase means is not the same as *you* understanding it. The disciples were hearing many words and often hearing understanding given with it. They could even *parrot* the words Jesus spoke, but in order to understand it the way *he* understood it would require a series of personal revelations. An "aha!" usually comes unexpectedly after much germination. The personal revelations of the disciples sometimes did not come for years. (See Acts 11:1-13)

Jesus also spoke of an even deeper depth of understanding, the **unitive/integral** (L4).

> I and my Father **are one**. (Joh.10:30) That they **all may be one**; as thou, Father, art in me, and I in thee, that they also **may be one in** us: that the world may believe that thou hast sent me. And the **glory** which you gave me I have given them; that they **may be one**, even as we **are one**; I in them, and thou **in** me, that they **may be made perfect in one**; and that the world may know that thou hast sent me, and hast **loved** them, as thou hast **loved** me. (Joh.17:21-23)

I use the Bible as a model of depths of understanding for those of you that have some Christian background. Each secular, scientific, and spiritual discipline has its own examples complete with teachers and disciples.

History is full of people receiving revelations after going through a process of preparation. It happens throughout the world today. Here is a mixed bag of how revelations happen.

1. **Archimedes** was trying to solve a problem. He had collected lots of data that was swimming round-and-around in his mind. While in his bathtub, relaxed, the data came together in such a way that he could *see* the solution he had been struggling to find. Reportedly, he shouted *"Eureka."*

2. Jean Houston tells the story of **a village in southern Africa** that used a process for acquiring a group revelation. Loosely: Whenever the village became aware of a problem that affected the whole village such as an issue with water or sewage or food or wandering elephants, they would all gather together, thoroughly talk about the problem and then drum, dance and sing—maybe for hours—until the group had a common vision (a revelation) of the solution.

3. *Apokalupsis* (apocalypse) is the Greek word for "revelation, lighten, appearing, coming." When you or I have a revelation, we are having *an apocalypse*. Wow! Yes! When the *light bulb* comes on our mind (after we have a question and have collected a fair amount of data), the answer can be *revealed.*

Many believe ***The Revelation of John*** answers the question of when and how Jesus will come again. Didn't Jesus already answer that question in Joh.14:23? *Apocalypse* has become a fearful 'end of the world' term. Whose *Old World* ends when they get a revelation? I don't know what question you are seeking an answer to and I don't know how disciplined you've been in collecting pertinent data. Is it time yet for you to take a bath or dance to the drums and sing with your village or sit alone out on an island?

4. **George Washington Carver** had a system for receiving revelations, a system that started to form the night he asked for a pocketknife as a young boy. That night he had a dream that revealed where to find it. The next morning, he ran to that spot and it was just as it was in his dream.

Many years later, he shared the perfection of his method. He deeply **loved** each flower, plant and piece of clay and truly saw them as direct links to the infinity of *God*. He knew he was no better than the flower and was in awe over each little piece of creation he was led to question. He would explain to the sincere seeker that he **loved** a flower so much that when he asked it questions, it would *reveal* to him its secrets.

He would confirm the revelations in his very modest laboratory before sharing each 'new discovery' with the world. In a sense, his example reveals to us how we will get revelations: be humble, ask our questions of someone or something we deeply love, listen for the answer, and apply it without doubt. Read his story in Glenn Clark's *The Man Who Talked with the Flowers*.

Were his revelations scientific or spiritual? Is there a difference? He clearly was a scientist and a deeply spiritual man. He saw no separation between the two.

I'm reminded of the movie ***Contact*** and the discussion Jodie Foster, the scientist, had with Matthew McConaughey, the minister. Her training indoctrinated her to believe only what she could prove. His training convinced him that you *can* know things without being able to prove them. He *won* the argument when he asked her to prove that she loved her father.

Science, especially physics, continues to **dig deeper** into the realm of energy (spirit). It can only be spoken of **symbolically** because only the product of its presence can be seen. Physicists are agreed that all energetic existence is **connected** and **interdependent** and there is talk of a **unified** theory of the forces of existence. They **dig** by asking questions. They are intent on understanding *how* it all works.

Spiritual seekers also ask the deep questions of life: "Why is there so much suffering in the world?" "Is there intelligent life in other parts of the universe?" "What do my dreams mean?" "What is my purpose for being here at this time?" "How can heaven be *up* and hell be *down*?" "Is the Universe living or dead?"

I believe it is healthy to have a questioning mind, unless questioning has just become another habit. So many people have a desire to find real answers to the above questions.

For an adult education class in the early 1980s, I devised **the 5 D's For Controlling Your T.E.A.R.S.** (thoughts, emotions, actions, relationships and spirit).

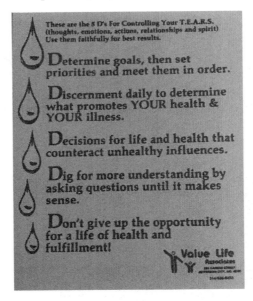

These are the 5 D's For Controlling Your T.E.A.R.S. (thoughts, emotions, actions, relationships and spirit) Use them faithfully for best results.

Determine goals, then set priorities and meet them in order.

Discernment daily to determine what promotes YOUR health & YOUR illness.

Decisions for life and health that counteract unhealthy influences.

Dig for more understanding by asking questions until it makes sense.

Don't give up the opportunity for a life of health and fulfillment!

Value Life Associates

Q. Who are the 5 Ds speaking to?

A. You, the observer and part-time decision-maker.

If you don't **Determine** a goal, you'll never have a problem getting somewhere or getting something done. Are your priorities flexible or rigid? How do you come up with an order of priorities?

Health might come naturally in a healthy environment, but where can you find that? Our mental and physical environments present us with significant challenges. Building the **Discernment** filter that will sort out the forces that promote life and health from those that promote illness can be tricky given all the 'expert' advice out there. I can't emphasize too much how important it is to carefully listen to your own body and to the intent of the thoughts that appear in your mind.

As I've said in other places, personal **Decisions** are somewhat rare given the amount of automatic behavior we engage in. All the more reason to value those moments and cultivate a motive that promotes life and health for all.

Dig for more understanding by asking questions. We covered that in the first of this chapter.

Suicide is seen by some as a solution to pain and suffering. I'm speaking to that when I say, **Don't give up!** Please, anyone contemplating suicide, seek a different alternative, unless there are no alternatives. In that case, rest in peace.

Over the years, the 5 D phrases evolved into the card you see below. Robots have no intentionality. I believe humanity can learn to shift from its automatic, reflexive, robotic behaviors to mastering the **Strategies for Intentional Living.** Any questions?

Strategies for Intentional Living

1. Determine from your yearnings a goal or project.
2. Discern your allies & your obstacles along the way.
3. Decide that you are the one that can & will do this.
4. Dig for more understanding by asking questions.
5. Don't give up on this possibility of a better world.

If it is to be, it is up to US!

Copyright © 2015 Value Life Associates

Swimming Hole #13

First graders learn what happens when you plant seeds by growing things on their window sills. It is also easy to show the relationship between plants and animals in that same class.

Maybe you were shown the Bell jar demonstration by putting a healthy plant under the jar only to watch it die. Then you put a similar plant under the Bell jar along with a small rodent and they both lived. It was **interdependence** in action without having all the deep understanding. What if that were taught in every classroom?

Along with this demonstration and discussion, the teacher could introduce five elements of the Periodic Table of Elements that every 1st Grader encounters every day. They all breathe. **Oxygen** in; **Carbon** Dioxide out. They all drink water. Add **Hydrogen**. They all eat. Carbohydrates and fats are already covered since they are made of the first three. Protein requires the addition of **Nitrogen** and brushing their teeth usually involves **Fluorine** in the fluoride tooth pastes.

The next year they could follow-up with the equation for **photosynthesis** which tracks Carbon, Hydrogen, and Oxygen into and out of plants and into and out of animals.

Children can handle two or more languages in these early years. Why be so afraid to introduce the science they can observe and understand at that age? I wrote an article titled, *"The Mystery of the Missing Table."* It's a Sherlock Holmes mystery you'll find in the back of the book.

And why don't we teach all students that ideas get planted in their minds and they can learn to discern which ones to keep and which ones to weed out? This lesson alone empowers them. Why don't we do more to reward questions from the curious and confused? Why? Why? Why?

14.

Sleeping Through a Great Revolution

Are you sleeping through a great rEvolution of Values?

Copyright © 2015 Value Life Associates

The 1960's

This Photoshop mashup of images simulates two speeches of Dr. Martin Luther King, Jr along with the British and Colonial flags of the Revolutionary War. Most people know or hear about the "*I have a dream*" speech from the March on Washington, August 28, 1963. Few hear about his Oberlin College Commencement Speech, delivered in June 1965. He titled it "*Remaining Awake Through a Great Revolution.*"

Dr. King was awake and revolution was underway in many locations, including his own mind. He used the story of Rip Van Winkle to set the stage. As Rip entered the tavern for a mug or two, a picture of King George III was displayed. He left the tavern, met some wee people who offered him a special drink, and fell asleep. When he woke up and returned, the picture of another George was displayed on the wall—George Washington. Rip had slept through a great revolution.

I was *asleep* in August 1960 working as a soda jerk in the town of my birth. We had moved back there the previous summer. One hot day, two young black kids came in and asked for ice cream cones. I said, "*Sure, have a seat.*" They wouldn't sit. I protested several times. With a fearful look, one finally touched the side of a counter stool with her hip. I handed them the cones. They slapped down the money and ran. I thought their behavior was strange.

Then I looked over and saw the owner/pharmacist giving me the finger that says, "Come here." He said, *"Dick, we don't allow black people to sit down in here."* It was a two-by-four smack to my mind. I had no place to put it. I had grown up with black women housekeepers and worked alongside black men hired as porters for my father's clothing store. I didn't know Blacks had to use a separate door at the movie theaters. If there were White and Black water fountains, I was blind to them.

That fall I met a girl from school at an ecumenical church meeting. We talked and I told her my story. We decided to find a Black church in that tiny town. It didn't take long and one Sunday morning, we were there. I don't know if we were the first and/or last Whites to attend, but they welcomed us joyfully and we had a good time. I wasn't *awake*, but I was starting to *dream*.

My family moved back to Columbia and I started college at Mizzou. The United Methodist Church Wesley Foundation tried to *wake me up* with visits to a couple of places where important social change was happening—San Antonio and the **Ecumenical Institute** in Chicago. We even learned about some of the community organizing being done in our own community.

I transferred to Southern Methodist University (SMU) in Dallas, TX to get away from home and arrived there in time to watch that August 1963 *"I have a dream"* speech on a black and white TV. Three months later, JFK was assassinated in Dallas. I was still in *dream sleep*, a nightmare. At the time, I bought into the Lee Harvey Oswald sham and went back to *sleep*.

The summer of 1964, I joined two Mizzou students on a month-long trip to Lima, Peru where I witnessed up close the most intense poverty I could imagine. Columbia had poverty that I had walked by, but I had never actually stepped into that neighborhood known as *Shanty Town*. When I returned home from Peru, I was suffering from culture shock and appeared so depressed to my father that he set me up with a psychiatrist in Dallas—a shallow experience.

I don't think I knew Malcolm X was assassinated in February 1965. Did I know who he was and what the Nation of Islam was doing? How could I have known when I was *asleep*? Two months later, I got a phone call to join a bus trip to Alabama; I *sleepily* said, "Sure." I had not been watching TV or reading the paper, so I had no clue what was going on in that state. We left one evening and arrived the next morning.

As the bus pulled up and stopped behind a row of buses, I learned we were joining the last leg of **the march from Selma to Montgomery**. Amazingly, my old Wesley Foundation director's bald head clearly stood out about five rows ahead of where we filed into place and I wormed my way up to join him on that historic occasion. I was ***there***, but I **really** didn't know what ***there*** was.

The next spring, my senior year, I got another call. *"Dalton, do you have a suit?"* "Yes." *"Can you be at the Student Center at 6:00 to join a few other students for dinner with a dignitary who's giving a talk tonight?"* "Sure." I suited up and was on time to meet Dr. Martin Luther King, Jr and ten other students for dinner. He and I were at opposite ends of the table and I could not hear a word he said. I thought I had too much homework to attend his talk. That's what ***sleepy*** does.

Unlike me, Dr. King was keenly aware of a great revolution of values taking place in the US and the world. Democracies were replacing colonial occupations as a world-wide voice demanded civil and human rights. Women's rights, rights of indigenous peoples, animal rights, rights of sexual preference and identity, and concern for the environment were streams waking up from the frozen glaciers of greed, fear, and male domination. It seemed as though the confluence of these streams could ultimately usher in a more peaceful and humane world.

On my way to Yale Divinity School the summer of 1966, I got my draft notice. They had not granted my graduate school deferment. With my father's help, I decided to enlist in the Navy. I went to **Hospital Corpsman School** at Great Lakes the next spring.

I was not aware that on April 4, 1967, Dr. King let the world know he had broadened his vision and his message. U.S. civil rights were important, but they were just part of a much larger picture. He said we must not let ***The Triple Threat to Human Rights of***

Militarism, Racism, and Materialism continue to violently destroy groups of people and force so many to exist in poverty, hunger, and involuntary servitude. He openly opposed the Vietnam war that JFK had tried to stop.

I might have been *awakened* at Yale, but the Navy sounded my reveille call by ordering me to compromise my values. **For the first time in my life, I had to take a stand.** As a kid, I had decided I would never carry or use a gun. I learned in Corpsman school that the Navy generals had decided to require their corpsmen, who were medics for the Marines in combat, to carry guns and act like Marines. When I got orders to Bethesda Naval Hospital, I let the chaplain there know, "I don't carry guns."

As I look back, I notice that the first part of my *waking up* was having my values challenged. I was willing to save lives and nurse people back to health, but I would not take a life. The next two years, I was in and out of the Navy brig on Treasure Island in the San Francisco Bay for refusing orders to Vietnam.

I was clearly not alone. Tens of thousands of others were taking a stand for their values. Each had a story that brought them to that decision. Many others thought I was unpatriotic to take a stand for my values, but I knew how devastating it was to kill a bird. I certainly could not kill a person. I can't say I was some kind of a saint. I was barely *waking up* to what was happening.

1970 - 2000

After getting my honorable discharge in 1970, I went **back to the land** in spurts during the early 70's. I also became part of Swami Satchidananda's **Integral Yoga Institute** and was teaching yoga classes in my hometown. I had even cut out an image of him seated in the lotus pose and had artfully set the image in a large philodendron in our living room.

In November 1974, I fell into a non-clinical depression resulting from my wife taking our very young daughter and physically leaving me. I was also *asleep at the wheel* when it came to relationships. One evening, seated on the couch, I had the distinct experience of *seeing* that Swami poster morph into the classic head of Jesus with the crown of thorns. I wept. My immediate interpretation said my values had just shifted back to my Christian roots. Depression can be part of *waking up*.

This shift from eastern philosophy back to my western foundation seemed like it required me to be a monk, like a friend of mine in Vermont. I contacted him. In the process of exchanging letters, a woman working at my father's clothing store—where I also did part-time work—was on her lunch break and offered to share a piece of chicken. I said, *"No thank you. I teach yoga classes and am a vegetarian."* She said, "I study the Bible." I said, *"Where?"*

Thus began 25 years with an esoteric, non-denominational Christian group just thirty miles away. My depression seemed to create the necessary environment for a *punctuated evolution* into *deeper depths of spirit* and understanding. The church pastor shared the first life-changing lesson almost immediately. "***Those thoughts you are having are NOT you. You are a soul. Those thoughts came into your mind and they can go out.***"

Of course, the explanation at the church for me even being there was *"God* brought you. You were called by *God* to be here at this time." I certainly had no better explanation. What are other teachers saying about events like this? What do you say? Was it coincidence? Synchronicity? The Law of Attraction? A pre-written script being followed? A happenstance?

Our *Minister of Understanding* was a woman. Elders were privately told she was the angel Gabriel. Who was I to argue. I became a 'clean' soul, learned to play the piano, wrote songs, was designated a music minister, learned I was a resurrected soul (having been Eleazar, third son of Aaron), preached, taught one-on-one Bible classes, worked in the 'gift' of discernment, got my masters and PhD in Health Education, got married again, and started a satellite group in our capital city where I got a job teaching at an HBCU. It took ten years. I dreamed I was *awake*.

2001: Deep Value Trend Analysis

In a previous Chapter, I told about my wife and I leaving the church in 2000 and my attendance at the 2001 **National Wellness Conference**. While there, I also met Dr. L. Robert (Bob) Keck. I went to his breakout session titled, *Deep Value Trend Analysis* and I was hooked. I bought his book, **Sacred Eyes**, took it home, and started reading.

Sitting on my deck, as I approached the end of the book, I had an epiphany—a clarity of understanding about my new role in the grand unfolding. ***I am like a cell in the body of the Universe doing my small part to keep it healthy and to nudge it with love toward evolution rather than destruction***. It may not sound like much, but I had been adrift for over a year after diligently serving twenty-five years in a ministry that taught that our little church was the 'Latter Rain' and we were called to 'clean up' the entire world.

Bob, himself an ex-Methodist minister, told his personal story and gave us the results of his doctoral research: an outline of human values divided into three epochs or time periods:

1. **Epoch I** (30,000 years ago to 10,000 years ago) he referred to as *childhood* when **humans valued**
    a. nature which was infused with Spirit;
    b. non-violence within and between groups;
    c. life and survival;
    d. physical development;
    e. women and worshipped a *God*dess of creation who was both giver and sustainer of life.
2. **Epoch II** (10,000 years ago to **now**) he referred to as *adolescence* when **humans valued**
    a. mental development;
    b. male domination of nature and each other;
    c. politics of fear;
    d. violence in competition;
    e. patriarchy as evidenced by worship of a male *God* and the domestication of women.
3. **Epoch III** (signs beginning in the mid-1900s) he referred to as *maturity* as **human adults began valuing**
    a. equality of all humanity in all categories;
    b. civil and human rights;
    c. cooperation over competition;
    d. democracies replacing colonial empires, occupation of other's lands, and dictatorships;
    e. spiritual development over religious rituals;
    f. a connection and interdependence with nature as celebrated by the first photograph of Earth in 1969 and the first Earth Day in 1971;
    g. thinking, speaking and acting with love.

This was the first time I had viewed human history through the lens of adult values. It put my church experience in a new light. We preached and practiced male and female equality, but fear of being 'out of order' was a more powerful motivator than real love. I believe we were part of the transition into Epoch III.

We look around today and see Epoch II values dominating the world. When 9/11 happened, I was not surprised. It was clear that most were not choosing their reactions; the fears and values imprinted as children reflexively took over. 'Independent' thinkers that challenged the media message provided by the government, were attacked as a threat to America. Nobody won.

Bob didn't know it when we met, but we were both dealing with prostate cancer. Sadly, he died just a couple of years later. Gladly, I could share his life and research with all my students.

Hair, the American Tribal Love-Rock Musical, opened on Oct. 29, 1967 in NYC and on Aug. 29, 1969 in San Francisco. I was in both cities when it was playing, but didn't see it until last year. I bring it up because of its celebratory song, ***Aquarius (Let the Sun shine in)***. The values associated with *the Age of Aquarius* are Epoch III values. Read through the lyrics, watch and listen to **The 5th Dimension** perform it on YouTube. It's invigorating, catchy, and hard to argue with. Where have you heard this message before?

Swimming Hole #14a

Some lines from *Aquarius* (Let the Sunshine in)

Then **peace** will guide the planets and **love** will steer the stars...
Harmony and **understanding**, **sympathy** and **trust** abounding
No more falsehoods or derisions, Golden living dreams of visions
Mystic crystal revelation and the mind's true liberation...
When you are lonely, let it shine on...
And when you feel like you've been mistreated
And your friends turn away
Just open your heart, and shine it on in.

Swimming Hole #14b

"**A true revolution of values** will soon cause us to question the fairness and justice of many of our past and present policies. On the one hand, we are called to play the Good Samaritan on life's roadside, but that will be only an initial act. One day we must come to see that the whole Jericho Road must be transformed so that men and women will not be constantly beaten and robbed as they make their journey on life's highway. **True compassion** is more than flinging a coin to a beggar. It comes to see that an edifice which produces beggars needs restructuring.

"**A true revolution of values** will soon look uneasily on the glaring contrast of poverty and wealth. With righteous indignation, it will look across the seas and see individual capitalists of the West investing huge sums of money in Asia, Africa, and South America, only to take the profits out with no concern for the social betterment of the countries, and say, '*This is not just.*' It will look at our alliance with the landed gentry of South America and say, '*This is not just.*' The Western arrogance of feeling that it has everything to teach others and nothing to learn from them is not just.

"**A true revolution of values** will lay hand on the world order and say of war, '*This way of settling differences is not just.*' This business of burning human beings with napalm, of filling our nation's homes with orphans and widows, of injecting poisonous drugs of hate into the veins of peoples normally humane, of sending men home from dark and bloody battlefields physically handicapped and psychologically deranged, cannot be reconciled with wisdom, justice, and love. A nation that continues year after year to spend more money on military defense than on programs of social uplift is approaching spiritual death."

Dr. Martin Luther King Jr April 4, 1967 Riverside Church NYC

15.

Meme Wars

On the 10-hour bus trip to the **Wakonse Institute** in May 2000, the Mizzou architecture professor from Israel listened to my story and suggested I read *The Evolving Self* by Mihaly Csikszentmihalyi. When I got home, I did. It introduced me to the term *meme* (rhymes with dream). First coined in 1976 by Richard Dawkins in his book *The Selfish Gene, meme* has since taken on a life of its own. I was inspired by the term, its meaning, and its vast application.

A *meme* is a piece of cultural information passed from mind to mind through social intercourse (communication). You can see the parallel to genetic information passed on by genes through sexual intercourse. Just as genes define the limits of cellular structure and behavior, so *memes* dictate all human social and organizational structure and behavior.

Genes promote an organism's survival. *Genocide* is the eradication of a specific gene pool. *Memes* compete to promote their own survival. *Memocide* is the intentional eradication of an idea or language. Both *genocide* and *memocide* are conducted by power-hungry *memes* that overwhelm their competition. This is the ultimate example of what a *Meme War* can do.

Humans depend on *memes* (words, ideas) to communicate. Jill

Bolte Taylor tells us in *My Stroke of Insight*, how she lost all words (*memes*) from a stroke. Without words, she did not *know* anything. She could observe with all her senses, but had no word associations to know what she was seeing. When her mother walked in her hospital room, she had no words to *know* who this person was. When her mother crawled into bed beside her and held her, she felt good, but had no words to *know* what was happening. Jill then got to selectively decide, as an adult, what to reprogram into her mind. Very few have that option.

Helen Keller's early emotional struggle, without having sight or hearing, occurred because she had no words (*memes*). She could not have had **Self-awareness** without accumulated knowledge (words). The excitement she experienced when the first *meme* (water) conceived in the womb of her mind at age five, would have led to the learning of her name and the birth of the **Self**.

As the first *meme* enters a child's mind, it becomes part of the emerging, self-organizing process of perception and communication. In *Out of Control*, Kevin Kelly wrote, "*self-replicating ideas or memes can quickly accumulate their own agenda and behaviours.*" ***Memes*** mutate and combine into belief systems, values, languages, songs, and rules that drive personal and societal behavior.

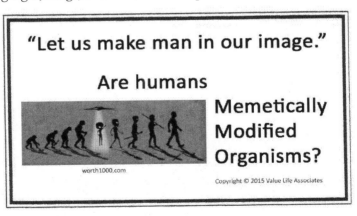

There are theories on the origin of *memes*. Ideas require words, so words had to evolve from body language or else be transmitted from another source that already had them. Chapter 3

of Genesis implies that **memes** were passed on to humans in the Garden of Eden by *God*, trees, and a snake (the *devil*).

Michael Tellinger wrote **Slave Species of the Gods** to pass on the **meme** that it was extraterrestrials who first genetically and then **memetically** modified higher order primates into what are now called human beings. Some would say that *God* and *god*s are extraterrestrials.

Others profess there is a Cosmic Consciousness (e.g. Universal Mind, The Field, Akashic Records) interacting with human consciousness co-creating the **memetic** inner world of mankind and, therefore, all its **meme**-made manifestations. This all leads to the observation that **memes** use the human mind to spread, mutate, and compete. Some **memes** go viral—they are so catchy, timely or clever that their mass appeal infects millions. I go so far as to entertain the notion that **memes** are invisible (spirit) organisms that first made their appearance some time in our distant past and have taken over this planet's human culture.

Inscribed in Missouri's Capitol Rotunda are these words: "IDEAS CONTROL THE WORLD." **Memes** are ideas. So, we could say **MEMES CONTROL THE WORLD** and humans do their bidding (follow their instructions). We could even say us **humans are slaves to our slave master memes** until we learn how to get emancipated and apply that knowledge. **Why do people do what they do?** Beyond automatic genetic reflexes, they are doing what an idea (**meme**) tells them to do.

Memes compete to dominate and control our thinking and behavior. **Memes** get us to fight and kill each other, do things we don't want to do, and treat each other badly. **Memes** also get us to cooperate, help the needy, and dedicate our lives to promote a healthier, more peaceful world for everyone. When we realize that *some* **meme** is going to *drive our car*, we can take a more active role in picking our *chauffeurs*.

Some **memes** tell us to focus only on the outward labels of color, ethnicity, age, religion, gender, political party, or sexual preference. If you saw Spike Lee's marvelous movie, **Jungle Fever**, you felt the power of **memes** to separate, denigrate, and condemn to the point of murder. People lusted or fought because of indoctrinated beliefs (*memes*) ingrained in their subconscious. Some tried to change their behaviors as life conditions changed, but a new idea *here* provoked an old value *there*. The *meme wars* were intense.

As you watched it, you may have felt your own *memetic* biases related to Blacks and Whites, shades of color, male and female, old and young, economic status, family relations, drug use, police and society, all in a stew pot of the city. I challenge you to examine the origins of your biases and decide if they contribute to a safer, healthier world for **all**. You **can** change.

While attending a **Social Artistry Leadership Intensive** put on by Dr. Jean Houston in Ashland, Oregon in 2005, attendees were captivated by the presentation **Dr. Don Beck** gave on *Spiral Dynamics*. I was particularly fascinated because he sees all human behavior as governed by what he calls v*Memes* or value *Meme* codes.

Don's mentor, Dr. Clare Graves, developed the theory known as the "*Emergent Cyclical Double Helix Model of Adult Biopsychosocial Systems Development*." They met in 1975 and worked together until Graves died in 1986. Color coding and the language of *memetics* was added to the schema by the time Don and Christopher C. Cowan published their 1996 book, ***Spiral Dynamics: Mastering values, leadership, and change***.

Don went on to adopt the Integral work of Ken Wilber and formed **Spiral Dynamics integral** (SDi)—a bio-psycho-social-spiritual map of human behavior and motivation. Throughout human history, individuals and groups of people have confronted changing life conditions and problems. This usually forced them to see things differently. As perceptions changed, their values changed. As complexity grew, the process would repeat itself.

"Conditions" create Problems of Existence. Humans adapt appropriate coping systems.

If the world is seen as...	vMemes	then effective people...
a state of nature,	Beige SurvivalSense	act like other animals.
mysterious and frightening,	Purple KinSpirits	placate spirits and join together for safety.
rough and hard like a jungle,	Red PowerGods	fight to survive inspite of others.
divinely controlled and guilt driven,	Blue TruthForce	obey rightful higher authority.
full of variable alternatives,	Orange StriveDrive	pragmatically test for options for success.
a habitat for all of humanity,	Green HumanBond	join communities to experience.
in some danger of collapse,	Yellow FlexFlow	stand alone to learn how to be free.
a single living entity,	Turquoise WholeView	seek the order beneath the Earth's chaos.

*Adapted from **The Crucible** by Don Beck & Graham Lipscott (2006)*

This table is one abbreviated way to exhibit the value ***Meme*** codes.

The ultimate goal of this theory is a healthy alignment of the eight **vMemes** presently active on the planet. The success of this theory will be evidenced by people respecting the need for a healthy expression of each value level in the communities throughout the world. This understanding is now being applied in organizations, schools, cultural disputes, and civil wars.

Don Beck was kind enough to send me a simple slide show about **Spiral Dynamics** that he called the "training wheels" version. I had already been teaching Bob Keck's **Deep Value Trend Analysis** (See p.138) with its three epochs of human history when I noticed something: the two gentlemen's graphics could easily be married and *the two could become one graph.*

"WE" Values   "I Values

WholeView

                 FlexFlow

Epoch 3 - Maturity

HumanBond

              StriveDrive

TruthForce

             PowerGods

Epoch 2 - Adolescence

KinSpirits

SurvivalSense

Epoch 1 - Childhood

You notice that the Spiral v**Memes** weave back and forth from *"WE"* to *"I"* to *"WE"*. Clare Graves referred to that as the "double helix" effect.

There is no blame in SDi. v**Memes** are culturally imprinted into children's minds and behaviors and move along the spiral in response to changes in life conditions. Values move from more *survivalistic* to more *global order* and *renewal* unless a calamity occurs that *drives* the person to downshift into a lower level v*Meme*. Leaders trained in SDi don't judge individuals, they discern the v*Memes* that *chauffeur* or dictate adult human behaviors from day-to-day. When individuals learn to see their own v*Memes* for what they are, they can honor them and, if necessary, find healthier, more harmonious ways to express them in the midst of people who are at other v*Meme* levels.

Memetics is the study of ideas and concepts viewed as "living" organisms. It is possible for us to understand this *meme* world and become more selective about what *memes* we allow to run our lives. **We are not our *memes!*** We definitely have *memes*, but they are not us. Until we learn to discern the difference between us and our memes, we do not even have limited freedom of choice—the *memes* are our slave masters. As we come to understand that *memes* are not us, our will is *released* to choose from the available *memes* on the menu.

All of us became so indoctrinated with our *memes* of politics, religion and personal identity that it seems next to impossible to separate our true **Self** from those ideas others foisted on us. I understand now that I am not my ideas (*memes*) and that I can decide to agree or not agree with ideas according to *my* agenda and not someone else's. I also realize that there will always be a *meme driving my car*, but now I can decide which *meme* will be my *chauffeur*.

It takes a while to get the revelation, but it is a concept that could be passed on to children and be reinforced throughout the education process. What a powerful tool to give a child! Are adults afraid or just uninformed?

Teaching this concept is not really a new idea. Jesus told some religious leaders that their ideas (*memes*) were fathered by the devil and they were doing what the devil told them to do (John 8:44). Paul wrote a letter to the Philippians (2:5) saying, *"Let this mind [system of memes] be in you that was also in Christ Jesus."* Even the lyrics to one of Bob Dylan's songs says,

> *"... it may be the devil or it may be the Lord,*
> *But you're gonna have to serve somebody."*

Swimming Hole #15

"In the beginning was the Word, and the Word was with *God*, and the Word was *God*." (John 1:1) A word is a piece of cultural information passed from mind to mind through social intercourse; otherwise known as a *meme*. [By the way, the "W" was selectively added by translators who had a pre-conceived belief that *logos* in this verse was God.]

So, it could read "In the beginning was the *meme*, and the *meme* was with *God*, and the *meme* was *God*." *God* actually is a *meme* and everyone has their own belief as to what God is. Atheists even have an idea of *God* that they don't believe in. Theists have an idea of *God* they do believe in. Each individual who uses the term "*God*" has their own unique idea of the what the word represents.

Sometimes a charismatic leader will put forth a slightly different image of the *God-meme* and draw followers. If the leader is driven by power-hungry *memes*, violence will be used to threaten people into serving the leader. Fear has been the most common motivator in gaining religious followers.

We don't know where the *God-meme* originated. It is interesting that it is usually deemed all-powerful and all knowing. That is enough for most to sign up to be a servant. The master-slave language appears throughout the Judeo-Christian-Muslim holy books.

All our nationalistic and religious wars are due to *memes* competing for domination. Why do people become soldiers willing to give their lives in killing other human beings? Is it a *meme* of patriotism, revenge, tradition, obligation, fear, or duty? People who refuse to fight or serve in the military are also led by their pre-programmed *memes*.

If the *God-meme* were simply a synonym for **Love** and people internalized the **Love**-*meme*, there would be no place for violence. We may well be in a transition time of making the **Love**-*meme* so contagious that it infects all of humanity. When that happens, humans will finally become humane.

16.

Four Depths of Spirit

4 Depths
of Spirit

Want to learn how to swim?

Copyright © 2015 Value Life Associates

Google *four depths of spirit* (in quotes). No results? Yet, it was one of the first biblical patterns revealed to me in my ministerial training in 1975. Since many of you reading have some flavor of Judeo-Christian-Muslim teachings in your own background, I thought this topic might be both interesting and even helpful. See what depth(s) of Spirit have been working in you.

Let's dive in. Ezekiel says in Chapter 40:2 (KJV),

> In the visions of God brought he me into the land of Israel, and set me upon a very high mountain, by which was as the frame of a city on the south.

The visions continue through to Chapter 47:1 where he starts describing "waters" that "issued out from under the threshold of the house eastward."

A man with a measuring line in his hand starts guiding him:

> 3 He measured a thousand cubits and he brought me through the waters; the waters were to **the ankles**.
> 4 Again he measured a thousand, and brought me through the waters; the waters *were* to **the knees**.
> 5 Again he measured a thousand, and brought me through; the waters *were* to **the loins**. Afterward he measured a thousand; *and it was* a river that I could not pass over: for the waters were risen, **waters to swim in, a river** that could not be passed over.

This vision is not as popular as the parable of the 'dry bones' in Chapter 37; however, when it is connected to three verses in John 7, a greater importance begins to take shape.

> 37 In the last day, that great *day* of the feast, Jesus stood and cried, saying, If any man thirst, let him come unto me, and drink.
> 38 He that believeth on me, as the scripture hath said, out of his belly shall flow **rivers of living water**.
> 39 (But **this spake he of the Spirit**, which they that believe on him should receive: for the Holy Ghost was not yet *given*; because that Jesus was not yet glorified.)

"Rivers of living water" (the Spirit) connect further with Eze.47:9 where the river *heals* and *brings life*. This depth of water (Spirit) coming forth from a believer's belly (mind) heals and brings life. Let's explore these four depths of Spirit (**D1-D4**).

> D1 = ankle deep = Breath of Life
> D2 = knee deep = Wading in the Word and Spirit
> D3 = loin deep = Power to Overcome Spiritual Slavery
> D4 = river to swim in = Love to Perfection

Breath is another word-picture for Spirit. In the second creation account, the LORD God "formed man of the dust of the ground and breathed into his nostrils the **breath of life**; and man became a **living soul**." (Gen.2:7) Science confirms that our bodies are made of earth. The *soul* and what makes it alive has not been defined by science. Biblically, all living things have breath (spirit) of life (Gen.6:17; Psa.90:10). This is **D1**.

In the context of the Hebrews and then Jesus and his followers, we find some people are "**moved** by the Holy Ghost" and called *holy* (2Pe. 1:21). Those receiving the **word of God** are even called *gods* (Joh.10:34-36). This "closer walk" with limited power of word and spirit is **D2**.

At thirty years old, Jesus was baptized by John in the muddy Jordan River. **D1** and **D2** are corruptible depths of Spirit (1Co.15:53). The muddy Jordan represented corrupted Spirit. John protested when Jesus came to be baptized. Jesus said it would fulfill all righteousness. The spirit of Jesus in **D1** and **D2** had been kept clean by his parents, by the scriptures he was taught, by the dreams and leadings of angels, and by his own realization of what he was called to do. Knowing his spirit would be corrupted on the cross—because it was prophesied he would be the sacrificial lamb taking in the sins of the Moses world (the first testament: Heb.9:15)—he was immersed in the muddy water.

He then went into the wilderness, passed his rite-of-passage test by the devil, and "returned in the **power** of the Spirit into Galilee" (Luk.4:14, 32). This was prophesied by Isaiah, fulfilled in Jesus, and passed on to his disciples (Mat.9:6, 10:1, Luk.10:19, Act.1:8). This anointed **Power** of Word and Spirit is **D3**. See 1Jo.2:13, 14; 3:8, 9; 5:18.

When Jesus had a deep conversation with his Father (John 17), he ended with this statement (v.26):

> And I have declared unto them thy name, and will declare *it*: that the love wherewith thou hast loved me may be in them, and I in them.

This is the **Love** depth (**D4**) or "water to swim in."

> 1Jo.4:16 *God* is **Love**; and he that dwells in **love** dwells in *God*, and *God* in him...
> 18 There is no fear in **love**; but perfect **love** casts out fear... He that fears is not made perfect in **love**.

Are these **Power** and **Love** depths available to people now? Many church leaders say they are not. They say people cannot stop sinning, cannot be perfect, or be like Christ in this life. *Those that believe this message of limited possibilities will see themselves and the world through those glasses.* They have believed a self-fulfilling prophecy.

This may explain why so many people live with hatred, fear, violence, and constant judging of others. It may answer why so many 'children of *God*' **never** seem to grow up to the fullness of Christ (Eph.4:13, 1Jo. 2:13). They appear to be trapped like the lost boys of Peter Pan who **believe** only Pan can fly (find his happy place). Maybe it is *time* to **change the message** that says *you can't, you'll never be able to, it's impossible!* What do you say? "Forget the 'maybe'?" If not **Now**, when **is the time to change your glasses?**

Many of us grew up with stories of a super hero coming to save the day by overcoming the enemy. I recall *Mighty Mouse* and the musical line from the cartoon, "*Here he comes to save the day.*" There was Superman, Batman, Luke Skywalker, the X-Men, and the list goes on. In each of these stories, someone else with special powers was going to save the common everyday people from the powerful enemy.

The Christian superhero is Jesus, Jesus Christ Superstar, who will come with special powers and save the world from evil. **Jews are still waiting for the Messiah** and **Muslims are still waiting for the Mahdi.**

Some say *he* is supposed to return 'soon' and those that believe in *him* will be "caught up" in the clouds leaving unbelievers behind and subject to Satan's whims. "Are you ready if *Jesus* comes today?" Fear tactics are common.

There are so many lines of thought we've been given to <u>disempower</u> us. **"Sinner" is your slave name out of ignorance and lack of skill.** It's time to drop that slave name with your eyes of understanding wide open and your special skills honed through diligent training.

How many times have you proclaimed, "*I can do all things through Christ which strengthens me*"? (Php.4:13) Does that include be perfect, stop sinning, love all your neighbors, and forgive yourself and all others whatever the debt? Can you stop supporting war, inequality, hatred, judging, violence, prisons, greed, poverty, and hopelessness?

Those that believe they **can** grow to perfection, to the measure of the stature of the fullness of Christ (Eph.4:13), **challenge the old slave masters** that have their people believing they are **sinner-slaves from birth to death.** Those that believe they can and will be Christ-like in this life get called uppity and tools of the devil. Do you *hear* what I hear?

Being a *Slave to lies* or **Free from lies** are two options. Of course, the hardest thing is getting the discernment filter right. Is it loving? Does it bring you joy? Does it draw the people you are with to be more understanding and loving?

If fear of something 'other' is an undercurrent in your life, find the **belief button** in your mind that the thought of something 'other' keeps pushing. Did you choose to believe that back when it first conceived? Did you understand then why other people said and did those things that hurt you or made you fearful? Do you understand now? Dig for more understanding by asking questions.

Who was left behind?

Who was taken and destroyed?

Copyright © 2015 Value Creation Press

A few years back, some religious groups shifted their fear tactics away from hell and on to being "*left behind*" when the '*rapture*' comes. The sadly popular "Left Behind" series by Tim LaHaye and Jerry Jenkins used the old strategy of playing on people's fears to sell their books. Some church leaders are still successfully using this tactic on their congregations.

The painting above depicts many people about to drown in a flood. In the background, Noah's ark is safely floating in the flood waters. Do you have the answers to the two questions on the card?

There are 'sister' accounts of this event where Jesus was using the Noah story as a parable for his *coming*. Mat.24:37-38 and Luk.17:26-27:

> As in the days of Noah were, so shall the coming of the Son of man be. For as in the days that were before the flood they were eating and drinking, marrying and giving in marriage, until the day that Noah entered into the ark, and knew not until the flood came, and took them all away (destroyed them all); so shall also the coming of the Son of man be.

You'll notice that "took them all away" is the same as "destroyed them all." The ones that are "taken" are the ones destroyed by the flood. The only ones "left" after the flood are those within the safety of the ark.

Is the requirement for being saved, to fear being *left behind?* Jesus said being *left behind* was good, not bad, and "he that shall endure unto the end, the same shall be saved." (Mat.24:13) Paul said, *"For God has not given us the spirit of fear; but of power, and of love, and of a sound mind."* (2Ti.1:7) The spirit of fear is our slave master in **D1** and

D2. Power, love, and a sound mind are the order of the day in **D3** and **D4**.

In 2001, I got to play "the Duke" in the musical, *Big River* by Roger Miller based on **Huckleberry Finn** by Mark Twain. The Duke is supposed to be a great Shakespearean actor, but is **scamming the unlearned**. At one point, he delivers the famous *"To be or Not to be"* soliloquy which is actually just a hodge-podge of lines Twain took from various plays by Shakespeare. Here it is in its creative fullness:

> To be, or not to be; that is the bare bodkin
> That makes calamity of so long a life;
> For who would fardels bear,
> Till Birnam Wood do come to Dunsinane
> But that the fear of something after death
> Murders the innocent sleep
> And makes us rather sling
> The arrows of outrageous fortune
> Than fly to others that we know not of.
> There's the respect must give us pause:
>
> Wake Duncan with thy knocking! I would thou couldst;
> For who would bear the whips and scorns of time,
> And the quietus which his pangs might take,
> In the dead waste and middle of the night,
> When churchyards yawn
> In customary suits of solemn black,
>
> But that the undiscovered country
> From whose bourne no traveler returns,
> Breathes forth contagion on the world,
> And, like the poor cat in adage,
> I sicklied o'er with care,
> Tis a consummation devoutly to be wished.
> But soft you, the fair Ophelia, Nymph
> Ope not thy ponderous and marble jaws,
> But get thee to a nunnery – go!

Many teachers and preachers take a hodge-podge of quotes to make their case and I have done the same thing. It is tough deciding what to believe these days with so many voices broadcasting the 'truth.' Building a discernment filter that keeps fear, judging, and disempowering ideas out of our mind is crucial.

Sometime after playing the Duke, I was inspired to put new words to his soliloquy. I think you'll see why I include it here.

A Traveler's Soliloquy – Fusion Poetry by Richard B Dalton
Mark Twain's "Duke" meets the "Left Behind" Series

To be taken away by the flood and destroyed
Or not to be taken and live?
That is the real Bible question
That makes a farce of the "Left Behind" threats;
For who would shun responsibility for our planet,
Waiting for a Messiah to come and whisk them away?
But the fear that they might not be taken
Murders the uninformed sleep
And makes them rather sling the arrows of self-right judgment
Than working with others that they know not of.
There's a thought must give us pause.

Wake the *God*s with thy knocking!! If only thou couldst;
For who wants to bear the waiting and the doubt
Not knowing if your sins may thwart your "rapture"
As you lay awake in the middle of the night
And wonder why
Your life is not what you had dreamed.

But there is a place perhaps you've not yet found
That other travelers happened on and will not leave
A state of peace and joy that draws you close to them
And if you let go of dogmas
You too will feel loved by the universe
And enter into the peace you've always dreamed of.
Yes you, my dear friend, fellow citizen of the planet,
Throw off the fears and threats of others
And enter into your passion – Now!

Jesus was all about **empowering people**. Growing **love** is coming to a clear and solid understanding that *you are **not** your thoughts* and the other person is **not** their thoughts. From Genesis 1 to Revelation 22, the four depths of Spirit create a useful framework. They describe limited to full access to the Great Mysteries. Many cultures tell similar stories replete with gods, saviors, angels, ancestral guardians, and healing powers. There is also common symbolic use of the four directions, four seasons, and four levels of development.

In his ministry, Jesus, as a Seer—Toltec level four—would interact and empathize with people in all four depths. He ate and drank with sinners, knew his history and what was in the minds of people. He always spoke symbolically in parables (Mat.4:24, 8:34) and taught **love** as the greatest of commandments (Luk.10:25-28). He healed the humble and told people to "be ye therefore perfect" (Mat.5:48) and "Judge not" (Mat.7:1).

What if each of us developed our own special powers of discernment, understanding, compassion, forgiveness, and love? There are also special powers of music, organizing, fund raising, public speaking, cooking, teaching, research, volunteering, listening, writing, healing, hugging, dancing, gardening, drumming, singing, coaching, and an endless list of others. All of these can be performed with **love**.

What does the world need to be saved from? Why would we rely on a single superhero to save the world when we all have or can grow special powers that will do the job when we work together.

"If it is to be, it is up to US!" My motto since 1991.

Swimming Hole #16

I was pleasantly surprised to learn what Dr. Martin Luther King, Jr taught about a phrase I had heard used much of my life. This is an excerpt from an essay he wrote while in seminary.

The Second Coming of Christ

It is obvious that most twentieth century Christians must frankly and flatly reject any view of a physical return of Christ. To hold such a view would mean denying a Copernican universe, for there can be no physical return unless there is a physical place from which to return. In its literal form this belief belongs to a pre-scientific world view which we cannot accept...Actually we are celebrating the Second Advent every time we open our hearts to Jesus, every time we turn our backs to the low road and accept the high road, every time we say no to self that we may say yes to Jesus Christ, every time a man or women turns from ugliness to beauty and is able to forgive even their enemies. Jesus stands at the door of our hearts if we are willing to admit him. He is far away if with ugliness and evil we crowd him out.

"The Christian Pertinence of Eschatological Hope"
www.kinginstitute.stanford.edu

Part Five

The Powers of Neutral and Longing

Somewhere over the rainbow, way up high
There's a land that I've heard of once in a lullaby.
Somewhere over the rainbow, skies are blue
And the dreams that you dare to dream,
Really do come true.

Someday I'll wish upon a star
And wake up where the clouds are far behind me.
Where troubles melt like lemon drops,
Way above the chimney tops,
That's where you'll find me.

Somewhere over the rainbow, blue birds fly
Birds fly over the rainbow
Why then, oh why can't I?

If happy little bluebirds fly beyond the rainbow
Why, oh why can't I?
Songwriters: Harold Arlen / E Harburg

This deeply powerful song expresses the faith that there is a "somewhere over the rainbow" and **a longing to be there**. This mythical story of the land of Oz, as is true of so many myths, ends up being about ways to make changes within our own minds.

One way to access 'a land that we've heard of' is to find the **quietude of neutral**—being without desiring. Another way is through honoring our longings and listening to their aches and yearnings. In fact, when we are truly quiet and shift into neutral, it is our longing that opens the portal to 'way above the chimney tops.'

A traditional symbol caught my eye and was explained to me on a recent trip to Morocco. A square represents earth. A circle represents heaven. When one square is placed over another so that it makes an eight-pointed star, it represents the in-between—heaven within you.

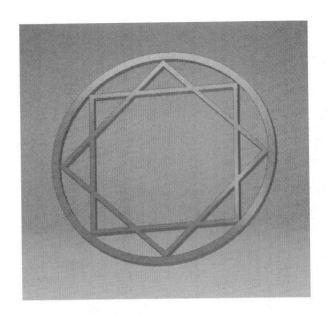

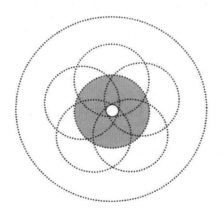

17.

The Sweet Spot of Neutral

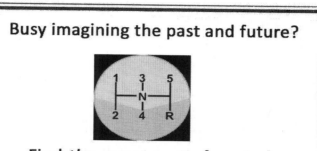

Copyright © 2015 Value Life Associates

A gearshift box, for whatever vehicle, allows it to 'get somewhere.' Just sitting in *neutral,* your vehicle goes nowhere. When viewed as a parable, I often call the vehicle that gets us around, our body. In this instance, **the vehicle is the mind.** The mind can travel all over the map in forward or reverse. What I have learned is that **neutral** can take me places no other gear can. I'm going to make a case for **neutral.**

So much of our lives is made up of **imagination.** Whether intentionally or reflexively by association, our past comes and goes 'a mile a minute.' There are good reasons to reflect on the past: 1) to forgive an injury, 2) to give thanks for all that has come before, 3) to honor the work that has so greatly contributed to our growth, 4) to remember a number, a place, a sequence of events, 5) to learn from a past 'mistake', 6) to tell a story for the benefit of others, 7) to write a book, 8) to learn about history, and 9) add some of your own good reasons that I missed.

Equally, **imagining** the future has great value and we all do it so much that I'm not even going to start a list. Of course, looking back and looking forward can be hazardous to our health. We can look back with regret, relive a hurt again and again, condemn someone in our past again and again, and justify why we are unable to forgive someone.

Imagining the future can also be stressful if it is all about some fearful *"what if"* that always has a bad outcome. I encourage you to **monitor your imagination** and take note of when it starts to shift from healthy to unhealthy (from planning to fear). Simply put, healthy feels *just right* and unhealthy feels overwhelming. Sometimes personal honesty in this area is hard to come by, but knowing that *you are NOT your thoughts* can give you a huge boost of power here.

For those that know the books, you may be expecting me to praise **Be Here Now** by Baba Ram Dass and **The Power of Now** by Eckhart Tolle. That would be a reasonable expectation because those books have helped so many of us along our journeys. I see those two books as encouraging people to focus more on the moment than on the negative past or future. Okay.

Victor Frankl told in **Man's Search for Meaning** how he survived the concentration camps by escaping the suffering of **Now** through his imagination. He intentionally shifted to thoughts of being with his dear wife in safe and loving *spaces*, not knowing if she was even alive. "But my mind clung to my wife's image, imaging it with an uncanny acuteness. I heard her answering me, saw her smile, her frank and encouraging look. Real or not, her look then was more luminous than the sun which was beginning to shine." (p. 58)

We do see the need for focus when driving a car or operating some other kind of machinery. And truly being present with a person or in a group allows us to listen without the background chatter of our **imaginations**. Other uses for the **now-*meme*** include attaining the *Flow* state that Csikszentmihalyi writes about. All good.

Neutral feels quite different to me. **Neutral** is more like non-focus. I'm sure You meditators have slipped into this state, maybe on a regular basis. I know I have experienced it a few times during meditation. In the back of this book you will find the **Warrior Meditation**. From its carnival scene on, the story was 'down-loaded' to me shortly after I slipped into *neutral* while meditating. When it ended, I was so thrilled, I immediately moved to the computer and typed it up.

I told you of the Jean Houston exercise when I became a Kalahari tribeswoman nursing my son (Chapter 11). That only happened because I slipped into *neutral* and stopped trying to see myself. It happened when I gave up—let go.

Another time, much later that same year, I was attempting to meditate in my basement. I must have *given up* when a young woman with short, straight dark brown hair and wearing a white 'karate' uniform rather quickly walked up to me, leaned over, and put a small 'present' in my lap.

Her expression was odd to me. It was a rolling-of-the-eyes reluctance that said to me, "*I'll do it if I have to.*" Only today as I type this am I laughing. Another student poster from class said, "We don't see people as *they* are, we see people as *we* are." The reluctance I saw **in** her was **in** me. What was *I* reluctant to do? And why? What **beliefs** make me 'reluctant'? That's one area in which I'll do some more exploring. Pause.

My initial exploration revealed that I'm reluctant to formally meditate regularly, even with these fruitful results. I'm reluctant to be *too* good or *too* bad, *too* right or *too* wrong, *too* busy or *too* lazy. I'm guessing this relates to my entire life history. I grew up acting the role of *good* boy while aware of **imaginations** I had that I was sure others labeled *bad*. I see that *this* could become a book in itself, but back to *neutral*.

For the record, the concept of *neutral* was given to me by the *angel* Gabriel—at least that is who we were told she was and we believed it. She was the minister of understanding at our church school in the 70s and one day, privately, she described how to 'let my mind go' and be in *neutral* so I could listen to whatever *God* had to tell me. It actually worked pretty well.

Long after Gabriel died, my wife and I left the group and I started to redefine and reframe things that I had believed during the ministry years. Big changes were happening in my beliefs, my philosophy of life, my relationships, and my body. **I was the same individual**, but my internal and external environments were evolving or, at least, adapting.

A student turned in her poster to health class one semester with a short quote from Rumi. It reminded me of *neutral*. He describes the place where two Souls can share their deepest connection. No censor. No self-right. No personal agenda. No point to get across. Sometimes, no words.

Neutral is also a state of mind when we can hear the cosmos, the Quantum Universal Mind (QUM), *God*, the heavenly spheres, the voices of the beyond. Remember, it does not come from trying to hear; it comes by letting go of trying.

So much of Rumi has *yearning* and *longing* and looking for or celebrating his male soulmate/lover/*God*, yet the following quote seems to hint there is a place beyond ideas of soulmate-lover-*God*. This place of *neutral* is very relaxed; nothing is missing and nothing is needed. No judging or anticipation here. Welcome.

'Out beyond ideas of Right-doing AND Wrong-doing. There is a field. I'll meet you there."
— Rumi
Sufi poet

Many speak of experiencing the presence of spiritual guides from another realm. I had read *Avatar*, the biography of Meher Baba by Jean Adriel, before arriving at **the Word church**. As I reflect back, he would sort of go limp for a time and later report he had joined a council of elders in another space-time-dimension. As a **pod of consciousness**, he might have *left* his body to do this. Many have had out-of-body experiences.

In an early 70s college psychology class, I read ***Center of the Cyclone*** by John C. Lily, M.D. The author's experiences with sense deprivation, Shaman-led journeys, and psychedelics included witnessing the movement of messengers back and forth from another dimension.

In the fall of 1973, I seized the opportunity of taking a TV class by John G. Neihardt called *"Epic America: Twilight of the Sioux."* Our text was his book, ***Black Elk Speaks***. The life and visions of Black Elk and their times together were particularly feeding to me. For a period of years, Dr. Neihardt would hold spiritual gatherings at his farmhouse focusing on opening contact with the spiritual dimension. He died in November 1973.

One of my church 'recruits' was reading ***Seth Speaks*** by the medium, Jane Roberts. The church called it evil spirits and/or evil angels at work. Anything that did not conform to their understanding of the Bible fell into the same category. With the multitude of expansive good things I received via that church, there were also limiting and damaging experiences.

I know, on occasion, I have received instructions for what to do in unexplainable ways. I had a dream that a woman and I were on our knees being married by the same Gabriel I've spoken of. At the time, I knew the woman, but didn't like her. I shared it with our pastor and within three years we were married, and still are.

Several times, I have learned of my future when I spoke it to someone else without making a conscious decision beforehand. The summer of 1971 while visiting a good friend on the Atlantic side of Long Island, we were out relaxing in a dinghy when I said, *"I'm going back to Columbia to start a Help Yourself Center."* The next day, I hitch-hiked back home and became the catalyst for the co-creation of several self-help groups using an empty space in a building my father owned. Part of the key has been the obedient follow-through.

In 2014, as my wife and I were driving home from a singer-songwriter weekend in Watttle Hollow, Arkansas, I spoke out to her,

"I'm retiring at the end of next semester." It was the first time either of us had heard *that* and I was not conscious of making that decision ahead of that moment. As it all turned out, it was perfect timing.

I imagine we all have messages come to us and through us that seem like *news* to us. I believe they appear during brief moments of *neutral*. Some teach that communications like these are *picked up* by our Right Temporal Lobe. Melvin Morse, M.D. calls it The *God* Spot:

> "We all have a *God* Spot, an area in the brain that permits communication with a source of knowledge and wisdom outside our physical bodies. Everyone seems to have their own definition of this source of Universal Knowledge. The Hindu religion calls it Brahman. Theoretical physicists call it quantum non-locality and the children I resuscitated from death simply call it *God*."
> http://spiritualscientific.com/spiritual_neuroscience/the_God_spot

Where God Lives by Dr. Morse was my introduction to this idea of the Right Temporal Lobe. It's another step by science in coming closer to understanding *God* (or the label of your choice). So many people throughout the world hear messages that seem to come from beyond themselves: dreams, premonitions, visions, songs, poems, and so on it goes.

Jean Houston and her father, Jack, overheard Edgar Bergen asking his wooden dummy, Charlie McCarthy, deep questions of life and Charlie answering with the wisdom of the ages that was beyond anything Edgar had thought or read. Neale Donald Walsch experienced his ***Conversations with God*** through automatic writing. Painters report that the brush seems to have a mind of its own. Inspired preachers/mediums answer specific questions of a parishioner without being asked. We hear of so many experiences of others, but may be hesitant to share with others various visions or words that we seem to *get* from the beyond.

Be still, and know that I am God. Psalm 46:10

I first heard this phrase in a Sunday School class on prayer when I was in high school. Then, it was a soft, inviting message to listen quietly and we would experience *God*. Now I look at the whole verse and it sounds bossy and pompous: *Shut up!*

> ... and know that I am God: I will be exalted among the
> heathen; I will be exalted in the earth.

Yes, I am now looking through a different pair of glasses, but I'm going to hang on to the soft invitation to experience ***neutral*** and see what happens.

I also believe we can be invited by another person to open our minds to this *God*-Spot. At a **Social Artistry Intensive** one summer, the incomparable Peggy Rubin led the group in a beautiful exercise. She set the stage by telling the context for Odysseus leaving home, his odyssey, and his return home—the Hero's Journey—taken from ***The Odyssey*** attributed to Homer.

Key verbs were offered on a worksheet: driven, drawn, traveled, suffered, struggled, etc. She said,

*"**The Odyssey** begins by calling on the Muse: 'Sing in me, Muse, and tell the story of ...'. Today, you will have five minutes—equal to all the time you need—for your Muse to speak through you and tell your story. You will start by writing that opening line, the request to your Muse, and letting your story flow onto the page. Begin now."*

Five minutes later I read my page to the group:

Swimming Hole #17

*"Sing in me, Muse, and through me
tell the story of the Godson man,
driven by an unseen knowing,
driven by the dreams of all ancestors,
drawn by the angel guides
and the wonderment of the world before him
to face and conquer
the fear of fierce judgment and subtle rejection.*

*He has traveled well the warrior trail,
the gypsy road, the seekers path,
and learned to listen and trust
with naive faith, the gentle nudge of God.*

*He has suffered the loneliness
of being an unknown friend to many,
the rejections of unknowing lovers,
and the hurts of yearnings unfulfilled.*

*His struggle to connect soul and body,
spirit and sensuality, love and surrender
have brought him to dance and weave
those dynamic poles of potent power
into a creative intention that connects
heaven and earth in every level of life,
and honors the awesome history
and the more awe-inspiring future
with every present moment."*

18.

The Lure of Longing

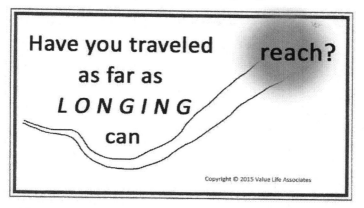

Have you traveled as far as *LONGING* can reach?

Copyright © 2015 Value Life Associates

"*Longing*" is such a potent word. What are you *longing* for or have you given up on whatever it was? The word conjures up things like being away from home, from family, from intimacy—unable to see or feel the familiar.

The question on the card has its root in a poem by the pre-Socratic Greek philosopher, Parmenides. *What is reality? Do we find it by rational inquiry or by the **intensity of our longing**?* Parmenides taught: the **intensity of our longing**.

Remember the process Georgy Washington Carver went through: his intense love for and *longing* to understand nature that took him beyond all rational inquiry. The same can be said for Rebecca Skloot and many others.

The **Self** *longs* to be recognized, to be acknowledged, to be *seen* and heard and loved. **Self** first believes *this* can be achieved by its appearance, ideas, and actions; but few are shown a pathway to even achieve the first ancient assignment: Know thy **Self**. I believe this book has offered a pathway.

> **Self** is the indivisible being (soul), observing its body, thoughts, feelings, relationships, spirit, and environment. **Self** can increase and decrease in its depth or level of awareness. **Self** makes limited conscious decisions when it sees it has a choice. **Self** can be fulfilled and even transcended in service to others.

As you walk by people, are **you** *longing* to be *seen*? I was at the movie yesterday with my wife and I noticed I was looking for people I knew. A quick scan easily dismissed a hundred people as 'unimportant' because I didn't recognize them. I was not practicing a friend's philosophy: "*I believe that every person I meet is important.*" Yep, **I** wanted to be seen. More work for **me** to do.

This sets up an interesting *test* I'll take with you: Notice how you feel when you look at people this week. Does your feeling change based on their clothing, hygiene, color, or obvious handicap? Does gender, age or ethnicity matter? What would it take to see and acknowledge the **Self** within all of that?

I know I still struggle with those on the corner or exit ramp with their various signs: "*Homeless,*" "*Need Help,*" "*Whatever you can give.*" They seem to be *longing* for something, something more than spare change or a few dollars. I know my money won't satisfy their *longing*. What to do?

There are huge needs around the globe, needs at every level of life. Even Mother Earth (Gaia) seems to be *longing, longing* to be acknowledged so that a healing process can begin. A part of each of us *longs* to help, but we know we, alone, can't satisfy what we see. The ***intensity of our longing*** will determine what we can accomplish.

Our men's chorus has sung a powerful song about *longing* as part of several concerts. You'll notice the word *longing* is missing, but the feeling of *longing* is unmistakable. It is about children in a war zone. It could easily be about any displaced person or someone whose environment has been destroyed by theft, fire, flood, bigotry, poverty, or governmental regulations. People pray to many different figures, but always with a hope that the figure will somehow help.

Prayer of The Children by Kurt Bestor

Can you hear the prayer of the children?
On bended knee, in the shadow of an unknown room
Empty eyes with no more tears to cry
Turning heavenward toward the light

Crying Jesus, help me
To see the morning light-of one more day
But if I should die before I wake,
I pray my soul to take

Can you feel the hearts of the children?
Aching for home, for something of their very own
Reaching hands, with nothing to hold on to,
But hope for a better day a better day

Crying Jesus, help me
To feel the love again in my own land
But if unknown roads lead away from home,
Give me loving arms, away from harm

Can you hear the voice of the children?
Softly pleading for silence in a shattered world?
Angry guns preach a gospel full of hate,
Blood of the innocent on their hands

Crying Jesus, help me
To feel the sun again upon my face,
For when darkness clears I know you're near,
Bringing peace again

Dali cujete sve djecje molitive?
(Croatian translation:
'Can you hear all the children's prayers?')
Can you hear the prayer of the children?

We *long* for fulfillment and for understanding the great mysteries. We *long* for the whole world to be at peace, to stop fighting, to get along.

A Facebook friend and former student of mine reposted a puzzle: *"Can you decipher the message? My mind is a mess that I can't escape."* I felt like he was *longing* to escape the mess. I commented to him about this book being available online. He wrote back: "U changed my life......thank u for your spirit."

It takes me back to Dorothy in the Wizard of Oz. "Somewhere over the rainbow, way up high; there's a land that I heard of once in a lullaby." Maybe that song was number one on the list of most popular songs of the twentieth century because so many people identified with that feeling of *longing*.

Longing and *yearning* are quite similar. When I presented the following card earlier in the book (pages 122-123), I didn't say much about it. Last year, the phrase *"from your yearnings"* found its rightful place in strategy #1. Why even have a goal or project if it doesn't come out of your deeper place of *yearnings*?

I borrowed "your allies & your obstacles" in strategy #2 from the *Hero's Journey* language. Putting the focus on "you **are** the one that **can & will** do this" is more empowering than the previous incarnations of strategy #3. Strategy #4 has not changed. Strategy #5 is broadened to include "this possibility of a better world."

> ### Strategies for Intentional Living
> 1. Determine from your yearnings a goal or project.
> 2. Discern your allies & your obstacles along the way.
> 3. Decide that you are the one that can & will do this.
> 4. Dig for more understanding by asking questions.
> 5. Don't give up on this possibility of a better world.
>
> **If it is to be, it is up to US!**
>
> Copyright © 2015 Value Life Associates

In 2002, my daughter recommended I listen to Jeff Buckley's cover of Leonard Cohen's famous song, *Hallelujah*. She had told me that Jeff had apparently committed suicide. His version stirred me more than when I first heard it years ago. Shortly after that, I was on a plane from Missouri to Oregon for a **West Coast Mystery School** weekend put on by Jean Houston and her staff. As I opened my mind, pen in hand, these words started coming together out of my subconscious connections and *elsewhere*.

For me, the song expresses a *longing* for us all to *acknowledge the sacred* in this whole amazing journey.

Hallelujah (tune by Leonard Cohen)

I heard my old professor say
in health class just the other day
"You don't really know how old you are, now do ya?
The atoms of dust, water, and air
were forged in stars before earth was there
when the sons and daughters of *God* sang Hallelujah.
Hallelujah, Hallelujah, Hallelujah, Hallelujah.

"A day with the LORD is a billion years
Conditions were right to make protein for gears
A double helix now turns it all into ya.
Inside us we have parts of all
The last descendants to hear the call
With minds and hearts to seek the Hallelujah.
Hallelujah, Hallelujah, Hallelujah, Hallelujah.

"But as we reach back to the stars
Our air is filled with filth from cars
And everywhere you turn they sock it to ya.
However there are those who care
For our earth, our food, our water and air
And give their lives to heal the Hallelujah.
Hallelujah, Hallelujah, Hallelujah, Hallelujah.

"We live in a present that's free to all
Take time to heed the inner call
Of the guides who over the years have been speakin to ya.
With words of harmony, peace, and love
With images of a descending dove
With interdependence in all the Hallelujah.
Hallelujah, Hallelujah, Hallelujah, Hallelujah.

"So now we join our hearts and pray
Each person in their special way
To live the dream the *God*s are bringin to ya.
And with every breath and look you give
Be grateful for the life you live
And share your love with all the Hallelujah.
Hallelujah, Hallelujah, Hallelujah, Hallelujah."

I'll end with the *longing* look of a young boy on a summer day around 1950. I believe it fits well as the final *Swimming Hole* entry. Raul Walters wrote this letter about a special day in our lives, just a year or two before his death.

Swimming Hole #18

"I recall a clear summer day. A group of boys and I, including the 'Dalton Gang,' were headed to the out-of-bounds quarry area. This old quarry had filled with spring water and by today's standard of danger from a one to ten it was a twelve!

Your son, Dick, was a little kid who somehow tagged along to this forbidden area. The boys became aware that Dick had slid down a rock bank that dropped straight down approximately four feet into the bright greenish-blue water. We all ran over to the area and did not see Dick.

The other boys held my feet and lowered me over the cliff. What I saw at that point is something I will never forget and that I have thought about many times since. Dick was about two feet under water and looking up with **his eyes wide open** and his arms and feet moving very slowly. The top of the water was not being disturbed at all and I don't know how long he had been under the water.

What I remember the most were **his eyes looking up**. The boys had to lower me down further. I reached down and grabbed Dick by the hair and pulled him up to the surface. He took a deep breath and without hesitation climbed up over my back and feet and over the chain of boys.

They pulled me up and after a pow wow, we made a pact — no one would talk about this as we were in trouble already for going to the quarry and we knew we would be skinned alive if anyone knew Dick almost drowned. As far as I know, that pact lasted more than fifty years."

Archives

The Gallery

Many of these cards I refer to as Provocative Parable Cards because the simple pictures reflect an easily understood message on the surface plus an esoteric story underneath.

[Esoteric: "designed for or understood by the specially initiated alone." Webster's New Collegiate Dictionary]

For their final exam, students in my *Mental, Emotional, Spiritual Wellness* class needed to explain and discuss ten of these cards. I thought throughout the semester that I was initiating them into the special language of the parables; but at the one-on-one final, student after student saw only the simple surface message. It was a good reminder to me that the initiation into deeper understanding is accomplished best through one-on-one—teach and give back—dialogues. Hopefully, the previous **Chapters** will effectively serve as our one-on-one.

The first cards were co-created around 1985 and others followed all the way up to 2016. No need to spend a great amount of time in **The Gallery**; I just thought you'd like to see them altogether.

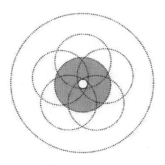

Do YOU ever do things
YOU don't want to do?

YOU   YOU

Which Y*OU* is <u>you</u>?

I am an Individual:
a unique, indivisible being (person, soul, entity)
connected energetically to all that exists.
<u>I have</u> a body, thoughts,
feelings, relationships, and spirit.
<u>I do</u> observe when I'm *awake* (aware)
<u>and</u> make decisions when given a choice.
<u>I follow through when</u>
I exercise my power of will.

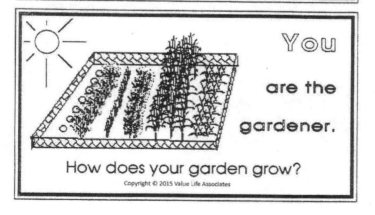

You

are the

gardener.

How does your garden grow?

Who were your gardeners?

What were they thinking?

Copyright © 2015 Value Life Associates

Who is driving your car?

Where are *they* taking you?

Copyright © 2015 Value Life Associates

"I have seen the Enemy and it is not US! You are NOT your own worst enemy!"

Copyright © 2015 Value Life Associates

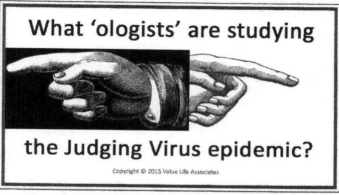

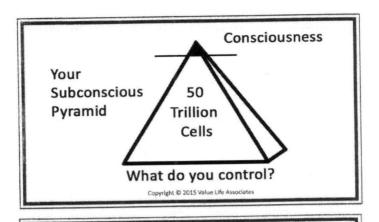

Consciousness

Your
Subconscious
Pyramid

50
Trillion
Cells

What do you control?

If "everything happens for a reason,"

why are so many happenings unreasonable?

Photo by Marc Riboud

Do you have any MIS-
conceptions?

Who is the "FATHER" of your thoughts?

The Parents who cried, "Wolf!"

"Grandma, is there really
a Jesus Christ and a God?"

Copyright © 2015 Value Life Associates

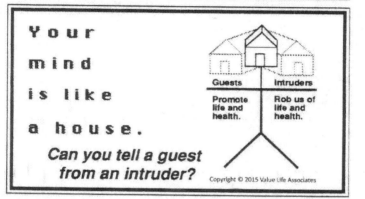

Y o u r

m i n d

i s   l i k e

a   h o u s e.

*Can you tell a guest
from an intruder?*

Guests	Intruders
Promote life and health.	Rob us of life and health.

Copyright © 2015 Value Life Associates

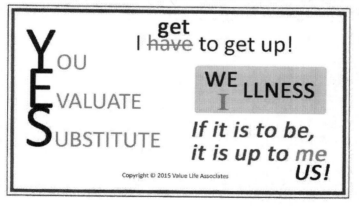

YOU
EVALUATE
SUBSTITUTE

I ~~have~~ **get** to get up!

WE LLNESS
I

*If it is to be,
it is up to me US!*

Copyright © 2015 Value Life Associates

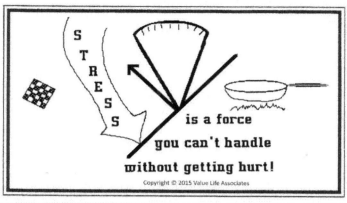

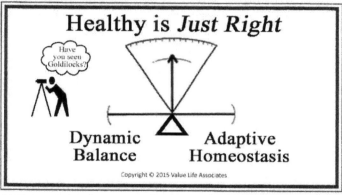

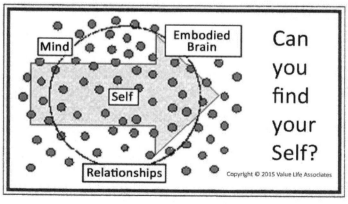

Circumcision?

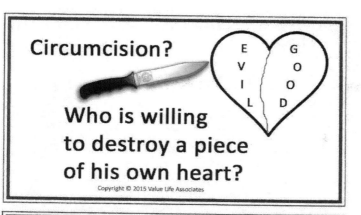

**Who is willing
to destroy a piece
of his own heart?**

Two wolves struggling in my heart.

The
Angry,
Vengeful,
Violent
Wolf.

The
Kind,
Loving,
Merciful
Wolf.

Which one will win? The one I feed.

**What Two Commandments
are written**

Love, love.
Luke 10:27
2Cor.3:3
KJV

in the fleshy tables of your heart?

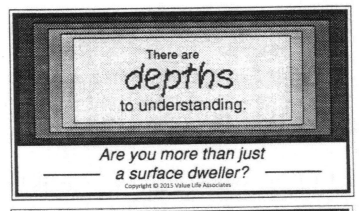

There are
depths
to understanding.

Are you more than just a surface dweller?

Copyright © 2015 Value Life Associates

Dig for more understanding.

Copyright © 2015 Value Life Associates

Strategies for Intentional Living

1. Determine from your yearnings a goal or project.
2. Discern your allies & your obstacles along the way.
3. Decide that you **are** the one that **can** & **will** do this.
4. Dig for more understanding by asking questions.
5. Don't give up on this possibility of a better world.

If it is to be, it is up to US!

Copyright © 2015 Value Life Associates

Busy imagining the past and future?

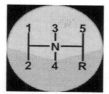

Find *the sweet spot* of neutral.

Has your G_{od}-Spot (Right Temporal Lobe)

been stimulated lately?

Have you traveled as far as *L O N G I N G* can reach?

The Social Artist

is one who brings the focus, perspective, skill training, tireless dedication and fresh vision of the artist to the social arena.

The Social Artist's medium

is the human community. She or he believes the creative capacity of the few can become the capacity of the many and that people can move from an ego-centric to an earth-centric world view.

One of Social Artistry's goals

is to create environments for people to become responsible (able to respond) to the demands of shared governance at personal, community, city, state, national and international levels.

The Social Artist

is trained to be aware of four levels of understanding and consciousness, and to consider each of them when approaching any situation or condition. These levels include:

- the physical/sensory realm,
- the psychological/historic realm,
- the mythic/symbolic realm, and
- the spiritual/unitive realm.

Embracing the work of Re-patterning Human Nature,

the Social Artist learns

- to think like a planetary citizen;
- to appreciate cultures & cultural stories & myths, while searching for the emergence of a new story, a new myth;
- to offer new models and paradigms of organization;
- to exhibit the joy of being a lifelong learner;
- to bring laughter and delight to learning and change;
- to serve as a healer of people and societies;
- to balance her/his life so that contemplation and meditation informs each action, and so that inward life and outward expression are complementary.

> **There is a prayer, a yearning, a longing, a cry for healing in the world.**
> **If it is to be, it is up to US!**

Social Artist descriptions are by Dr. Jean Houston. In a nutshell:

"Social Artistry is the art of enhancing human capacities in the light of social complexity." **J.H.**

Warrior Meditation

Sit or lie down in a position so that you can fully relax and not be distracted by your body. We will start out with progressive relaxation. Eyes closed. Cross your feet at the ankles and press your ankles together. Hold it. Squeeze. Hold. Now relax and place your other ankle on top. Press your ankles together. Hold it. Squeeze. Hold it. And release. Return to your most comfortable position making sure the soles of your feet are not on the floor.

Now focus your attention on your buttocks. Tighten the buttocks. Hold. Smile. Hold. And relax. Once again: Squeeze the buttocks. Hold. Smile. Hold. And relax. Allow any remaining tension from the waist down to dissipate into the floor.

Bring your attention to your shoulders. Bring them up toward your ears. Hold it. Hold it. And relax. Once again. Shoulders up toward the ears. Hold it. Hold it. And relax. Gently roll your shoulders forward and backward.

Bring your attention to your face. Scrunch all of the muscles of your face to the point of your nose. Make a prune face. Pucker up. Hold it. Now open your eyes and mouth wide as you say, "What's uuuuuuup!" Again, scrunch all the muscles of your face to the point of your nose. Make a prune face. Pucker up. Hold it. Now open your eyes and mouth wide as you say, "What's uuuuuuup!" Close your eyes now, reach up and gently massage some parts of your face, head or ears.

Now bring your hands together in front of you hooking them together securely like claws as you try to pull them apart without releasing. Pull. Pull. And relax. Now put the palms together and push. Push. Push. And relax. If you're sitting, rest your hands in your lap. If you're lying down, relax the arms beside you in the corpse pose.

Bring your attention to your breath. For abdominal or bellows breathing, imagine the hole for filling a balloon is right behind your nostrils collecting all the air you breathe in and the bell of the balloon is right behind your belly-button. As you breathe in, you fill up the balloon and your belly pooches out. As you exhale, the balloon empties and your tummy comes in. You can place your hand over your belly button

183

and monitor how well you are doing. Now, everyone, exhale, and breathe in—2—3—4 and out—2—3—4 and in—2—3—4 and out—2—3—4. Continue on your own, finding your own comfortable pace. You can soon forget about your breathing as you continue inhaling and exhaling through your nose throughout the exercise.

We'll now do some guided imagery as I shift into 1st person and my voice becomes your voice.

My eyes are closed and I am in that place between sleep and waking. I realize I've had a vivid and meaningful dream and as my eyes remain closed I'm able to go back and experience the dream again.

I am at a huge carnival with all the rides and hawkers calling out to me to try their ride or their game so I can win the big prize. Sounds of every kind assault my ears until they blend into a background hum. I pick a ride and round and round I go and where I'll stop, everybody knows, because it is just a ride and I have to get off.

Cotton candy, caramel apples, snow cones and all the regular carnival treats call to my eyes and nose and taste buds. I pick my favorite and savor the flavor. After a while it is clear that it's all fun and games, but it isn't satisfying a deep yearning I have. I decide to leave.

Somehow, I find myself in a desert just as the sun is about to come up behind me. I need to find some safety from the heat and I see a patch of green not too far in front of me. As I walk closer, I see it is a very tall hedge so thick I can't get through. I soon notice a happy-looking person standing by a narrow passageway saying, "**Welcome, we're so glad you made it in time, come right in and make yourself at home.**"

As I enter, it opens into a very large courtyard with an assortment of people walking, talking, reading, writing, playing instruments, even sitting in meditation. It's hard to tell what is going on, but actually it feels safe and peaceful.

An elder approaches me. "Ah, I see you've made it. We're always excited when the student is ready for their Warrior training. Everything is prepared for your journey. Walk with me; I'll show you around. Here is our small, but more than adequate library. Over *there*, classes are going on. Some, over in <u>that</u> area, are training for their special craft.

"You'll notice a lot of one-on-one conversations taking place. It is common for Masters to mingle with the trainees for special guidance, encouragement and to help with any questions you might have.

"I have 3 things for you that will be of great assistance during your journey. First is your cloak. As you will soon notice, it is tuned into your thoughts and feelings. It is for your comfort, protection, and most uniquely, for your transparency. Not to worry. Only Seers are able to see through the cloak. Any questions?"

Yes, what's a Seer.

"Ah, yes, a Seer is one step beyond a Master. Hmm. But, maybe I am getting a little ahead of myself. Why don't we go sit in on this class that's about to begin?"

Welcome, Class. Do you ever do things you don't want to do? *Lots of hands go up.* **Why do you do those things?** *People start speaking out answers*: "To get paid." "It's tradition." "Somebody's got to do it." "It's my job." "To be accepted." "I have to." *As they answer, I see that I'm not too different than the others here.*

Why don't you want to do them? *Again, people start speaking up and this time I join in with them*: "It's boring." "It's dangerous." "I hate it." "It doesn't pay enough." "It's not really my job, but I have to do it."

Are you happy when you do things you don't want to do? *Everybody says,* "No!" **Is it healthy for you? Probably not.**

Okay, class, you understand the situation pretty well already, so here's the big question: Which Y*OU* is you?

Just as the teacher says this, my tour guide hands me a beautiful notebook with a woven cover, saying, "I need to tend to some others. Whenever you are done here, we will continue. You may keep the notebook. I am sure it will come in handy."

I try to get back into the class, but I'm too distracted. Where am I? What are all these people doing? I have to get up and leave for a bit. I go over to the library. I need to do this at my own pace.

It's a pretty small collection of books and one quickly catches my attention: **The Fifth Agreement.** *I immediately wonder what the first four agreements are.* The <u>Table of Contents</u>: In the Beginning...Symbols & Agreements...The Story of You... *Ah, here they are: 1, 2, 3, and 4. The First Agreement is* **Be impeccable with your word.** *I need to look up the word impeccable. The Second Agreement is* **Don't take anything personally.** *That's impossible. The Third Agreement,* **Don't make**

assumptions. *Right, it makes an ass out of you and me. And The Fourth Agreement*, **Always do your best**. *I think this book is a little over my head.*

Part 2. *Ah-ha*, **The Fifth Agreement: Be skeptical, but learn to listen**. *What am I supposed to be skeptical of?* Dream of the 1st Attention. *Now they're dealing with dreams.* **The Victims**. *Victims? Sounds like a horror story.* Dream of the 2nd Attention. **The Warriors**. *The Warriors? My tour guide said this is warrior training. I wonder if there's a connection.* Dream of the 3rd Attention. Hmm... **The Masters**. *Ohhh. I'm on to you now. Maybe this book is like a script for a play or something. I'm like part of the cast. It better not be like The Hunger Games. I'm not really an expert in much of anything.*

Becoming a Seer. *Yep. I've got to read this book and see what's really going on here. I'm going through my dream and it's about dreams and levels and fighting and mastery. Pretty cool, actually.* **Epilogue: Help me change the world**. *Hmmm. I didn't expect that. They're asking for help. Not* <u>much</u> *help. Just help to change the world! Hmm... I wonder if this book even exists. I'll write it down in my notebook.* **The Fifth Agreement.**

"Hello." *Oh, Hi. You caught me skipping class. Just thought I'd check out the books in the library.*

"You did exactly what you needed to do—follow your own leading."

Hey, I think I'm on to you. I'm going to read **The Fifth Agreement**. *What are you smiling about?*

"I love you, Dear One. You are learning very fast. I think I need to share just a little more with you, now that you've started talking to two of our Seers."

I've only talked to you. And a little to the teacher in class.

"Two of our **Seers** wrote the book that has caught your attention. A **Seer**, as they explain, is a <u>Messenger of the Great Mystery</u> and this book is one of their messages. Let's see, you've probably heard of Maslow's Hierarchy. Their **Master** would correspond to the step in the Hierarchy called Self-actualization. But before he died, Dr. Maslow added one more step. He called it Self-Transcendence. The **Seer** has attained that level.

"You are here to examine the ways we all grew up as **The Victim**. You will be given tools here to release yourself from that prison and become the authentic <u>you</u> that I see hidden away in there.

"**The Fifth Agreement** tells us to **Be skeptical, but learn to listen**. Be skeptical of all teachings, all beliefs, assumptions and interpretations you have stored away in your subconscious and skeptical of all you hear and read and see from now on. Develop a new discernment filter for what you want to have working in your mind; then, only accept in and speak out what passes through your filter.

"Your training will take a while. For some, it took years. I was an eager learner, but I was rather slow in evolving my discernment filter. My teachers were patient.

"I know all this is taking place in your dream, but let me assure you, the dream is very real, real beyond what those around you call reality. Most of those in your everyday world cannot see past your cloak into your new reality. Some day they will follow their own yearnings. Someday, <u>you</u> will be a **Master** and then, a **Seer**.

"You will wake up soon in your bed and you probably will not remember all of the dream. That is expected. You are in **Warrior** training and you will start to notice there are more than a few **allies** eager to assist you.

"You will remember three words when you wake up. You will benefit from these three words as you apply them in your life. You need **Humility** throughout the rest of your journeys. You need help and it takes **Humility** to be able to ask for that help. With **Humility**, you will always know that you did not make it through the journey alone.

"**Honesty**. It's harder to live than you might think. You've been lied to by most of those in your journey so far. They weren't always intentionally lying, but they were not able to understand the deeper reality of who they were or what they were serving. You'll learn to live in **Honesty** clothed with **Humility**. You'll share, only when you are asked.

"You have already exhibited **Courage**. **Courage** takes you through the dark nights and allows you to talk to those that seem to be against you. You can begin to learn from every encounter. That **Fifth Agreement** also said: <u>Learn to listen</u>. Listen for the truth that may even be wrapped in filth, anger or hatred. Any questions?"

You said earlier that you would give me three things. You gave me this amazing cloak and the beautiful notebook. Was there really one more thing?

"Thank you for reminding me. Yes, the third gift. You will need a source of light during your journey due to the dark days you will experience. The most powerful light I can give you is waiting for you in the pocket of the notebook's woven cover. I assure you, it will not fail you. Any other questions?"

Will I be seeing you again?

"Well, I *am* in your dream now. How shall I put it? Yes, of course; honesty, honesty. You could not know it before, but I am one of your Dear Friends. I have always been with you, watching over you. My heart nearly came out of my chest when you finally saw me. I love you so very much and, yes, you **will** see me again. But now, it is time for me to go."

As the dream starts to fade, I quickly find the pocket on the notebook cover and reach in with my fingers. It is flat and smooth. As I slip it out, my jaw drops. **It's a mirror.** <u>The light will be in the mirror.</u>

I wake up as tears run down my cheeks. Thank you, my Dear Friend. I'm ready for training.

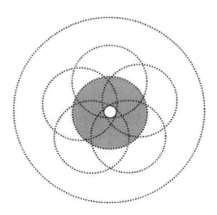

Bibliography

Adriel, J. *Avatar: The Life Story of Avatar Meher Baba.* Berkley: John F. Kennedy University Press, 1971

Assagioli, R. *The Act of Will-A Guide to Self-Actualization and Self-Realization.* Great Britain: Turnstone Press, 1974

Beck, D.E. and Cowan, C.C. *Spiral Dynamics: Mastering values, leadership, and change.* United Kingdom: Blackwell, 1996

Capra, F. *The Tao of Physics-An Exploration of the Parallels Between Modern Physics and Eastern Mysticism 3rd Ed.* Boston: Shambhala, 1991

Casarjian, Robin. *Forgiveness: A Bold Choice for a Peaceful Heart.* New York: Bantam Books, 1992

Clark, G. *The Man Who Talked with the Flowers-The Intimate Life Story of Dr. George Washington Carver,* Saint Paul: MACALESTER PARK, 1939

Csikszentmihalyi, M. *The Evolving Self-A Psychology for the Third Millennium.* New York: Harper-Collins, 1993

Dass, B.R. *Be Here Now.* San Cristobal: The Lama Foundation, 1971

Dawkins, R. *The Selfish Gene.* Oxford: Oxford University Press, 1976

Dodd, R. *The Toltec Secret to Happiness.* Hampton Roads Pub, 2014

Eliot, R.S. and Breo, D.L. *Is It Worth Dying For?* Bantam Books, 1989

Ehrmann, M. *Desiderata.* 1927

Frankl, V.E. *Man's Search for Meaning.* Pocket Books, 1963

Fromm, Erich. *The Art of Being.* United Kingdom: Little, Brown Book Group, 1993

Fry, C. *A Sleep of Prisoners.* NY: Dramatists Play Service, Inc. 1951

Griffin, J.H. *Black Like Me.* USA: Houghton Mifflin Harcourt, 1961

Houston, J. *The Wizard of Us-Transformational Lessons from Oz.* New York: Atria Books, 2012

Keck, L.R. *Sacred Eyes.* Boulder: Synergy Associates, Inc., 1992

Keith, A.N. *Three Came Home.* Boston: Little, Brown & Co., 1947

Kelly, K. *Out of Control-The New Biology of Machines, Social Systems, and the Economic World.* Massachusetts: Addison-Wesley, Paperback, 1995

King, M.L. "The Christian Pertinence of Eschatological Hope," and "Beyond Vietnam." www.kingencyclopedia.stanford.edu

Langer, Ellen. *Mindfulness.* USA: Da Capo Press. "A Merloyd Lawrence book", 1989

LaHaye, T. and Jenkins, J. *Left Behind*. Carol Stream: Tyndale House, 1995

Lily, J.C. *Center of the Cyclone-An Autobiography of Inner Space*. New York: Julian Press, 1972

Lipton, B. *The Biology of Belief*. Carlsbad: Hay House, 2006

Lipton, B. and Bhaerman, S. *Spontaneous Evolution*. Hay House, 2009

Mate, G. "How to Build a Culture of Good Health." YES! Magazine, Nov. 2015

Mate, G. *In the Realm of Hungry Ghosts: Close Encounters with Addiction*. Berkley: North Atlantic Books, 2008

McDonough, W. and Braungart, M. *Cradle to Cradle*. China: North Point Press, 2002

Milliss, I. "The Invisible Artist." *Identity & Anonymity: An Artful Anthology* (2016): 2-4.

Morse, M. *Where God Lives-The Science of the Paranormal and How Our Brains Are Linked to the Universe*. New York: Harper One, 2000

Morsela, E. "What is a Thought." *Psychology Today*, Feb. 2012

Neihardt, J.G. *Black Elk Speaks-Being the Life Story of a Holy Man of the Oglala Sioux*. Albany: State University of New York Press, 1932

Peale, N.V. *The Power of Positive Thinking*. Simon and Schuster, 1952

Quinn, Daniel. *Ishmael*. USA: Bantam Books, 1992

Robert, J. *Seth Speaks-The Eternal Validity of the Soul*. New York: Bantam Books, 1974

Robison, J. and Carrier, K. *The Spirit and Science of Holistic Health*. Indiana: Authorhouse, 2004

Ruiz, M. and Ruiz, J. *The Fifth Agreement*. San Rafael: Amber-Allen, 2010

Selye, H. "Stress." The Rotarian Magazine, March, 1978

Simon, N. *Fools, A Comic Fable*. Samuel French, 1981

Skloot, R. *The Immortal Life of Henrietta Lacks*. New York: Broadway Paperbacks, 2010

Szegedy-Maszak, M. "Mysteries of the mind: Your unconscious is making your everyday decisions." *U.S. News and World Report (Feb. 28, 2005)*

Talbot, J., Fandrich, L., and Specht, S.M. *Identity & Anonymity: An Artful Anthology*. New York: Mizzentop Publishing, 2016

Taylor, J.B. *My Stroke of Insight-A Brain Scientist's Personal Journey*. New York: Viking, 2008

Tellinger, M. *Slave Species of the Gods-The Story of Humankind from the Cradle of Humankind*. Johannesburg: Zulu Planet, 2005

Tolle, E. *The Power of Now-A Guide to Spiritual Enlightenment.* Vancouver: Namaste, 1999

Twain, M. *Huckleberry Finn.* US: Chatto & Windus/Charles L. Webster & Co., 1985

Walsch, N.D. *Conversations with God-An Uncommon Dialogue.* New York: G.P. Putnam's Sons, 1996

Young, W.P. *The Shack.* Los Angeles: Windblown Media, 2007

Bible Verses:
Gen.1; 2:7; 6:17;
Deu.30:6;
Psa. 46:10; 90:10;
Pro.24:9;
Eze.40:2; 47:1-9;
Mat.4:24; 5:48; 6:9-12; 7:1; 8:34; 9:6, 10:1; 12:43-45; 13:23; 18:21-22; 24:37-38; 26:31-46;
Mar.12:28-31;
Luk.4:14, 32; 8:10, 15; 10:19, 25-28; 17:21, 26-27; 23:34;
Joh.7:37-39; 8:44; 10:30, 34-36; 14:19-23; 17:21-26;
Acts 11:1-13;
Rom.1:20;
1Co.7:19, 15:33;
Eph.4:11-16; 6:17;
Php.2:5; 4:13;
2Ti.1:7;
Heb.9:15;
2Pe. 1:21;
1Jo.2:13,14; 3:8,9; 4:16,18; 5:18

The Mystery of the Missing Table

"It's Elementary, my dear Watson."

a short-story by

R. B. Dalton

1

"Holmes, did you see the story in the Times concerning the missing table?"

"I did not, Watson. Tell me what you read."

"Well, Sir, I found it a bit confusing. I'm not sure I can satisfactorily explain what the situation is. I was hoping you might be able to help."

"Come now, Watson, just give the basic elements: *when* was it discovered *who* was missing *what* table from *where*?"

"Yesterday, a local University Professor, reported the periodic table missing, from the elementary classrooms throughout the country."

"The periodic table? I was not aware that the periodic table was ever in elementary classrooms."

"That's what confused me, Sir. The professor called it the 'periodic table,' but the only periodic table I am familiar with is the Periodic Table of Elements and I was not introduced to *that* table until Middle School. I didn't understand it even then."

"Hmmm. Possibly he is referring to some other kind of table with periodicity. Indeed, the Periodic Table of Elements is, presently, the only table I know that describes itself with the adjective 'periodic.' And, as you indicated, *that* table would indeed be challenging both for elementary teachers and students alike."

"And another strange element to this story is the timing. In all these years, no one else has ever reported this 'table' to be missing . Don't you also find that to be a bit odd?"

"Very good, Watson. Yes, how could a 'periodic table' be missing from elementary classrooms throughout the entire country, and yet, not be reported missing until now? Unless."

"Unless *what*, Sir?"

"Unless the table was never there to begin with."

"Then why would the professor report it to be missing?

"That is the mystery we must solve, Watson. Why would a university professor risk his job and reputation announcing a table to be missing that was possibly never there to begin with?"

"So, you believe this man sanely and sincerely thinks that a periodic table is indeed missing from all elementary classrooms even though it might never have been there?"

"I give the man the benefit of your doubt, Watson. We must meet with this fellow, but we will be prepared. I would not want to appear ignorant conversing with the professor about whichever 'periodic table' he alleges to be missing; therefore, we must do some preliminary research of our own by exploring alternate tables with periodicity."

"If you say so, Sir. I suppose I could do an internet search for 'tables'."

"Excellent, Watson. My curiosity concerns the 'periodic' aspect of this missing 'table'. No doubt we will be able to deduce the very 'periodic table' of his charge at our next meeting."

2

"Let's see: www.refdesk.com; American Heritage Dictionary; definition: table. Nine hundred and nine entries!? This may take all night. Oh well, the variety of perspectives should prove valuable."

sand table
A **table** with raised edges, used for holding sand with which children play.

"Ah ha. Already success. Children playing at a table. But I'm at a loss in discerning any periodic quality of a 'sand table'. Next."

steam table, **training table**, **end table**, **night table**, **dressing table**, **Lord's table**, **coffee table**, **pool table**, **multiplication table**

"No obvious order to these entries, but we've moved from tables with legs to a table on a piece of paper. And this last definition looks interesting:

A **table**, used as an aid in memorization, that lists the products of certain numbers multiplied together, typically the numbers 1 to 12.

"This reminds me of another article I read concerning students in college unable to multiply without the aid of a calculator. The professor is possibly saying that calculators have replaced the multiplication table; therefore, the multiplication table is now missing from all elementary classrooms. This is too easy. Holmes will be impressed, but I best look further so as not to overlook another worthy candidate."

contingency table, roundtable
a. Arthurian legend, the circular **table** of King Arthur and his knights. b. The knights of King Arthur considered as a group....

"We've seen tables with four legs, tables on paper, and now two-legged tables. The variety is astounding."

sucre, livre, pya, leone, millime

"And now a Table of Currency. Page after page of different kinds of money. Next. Next. Next. Next. Ah, finally, the simple term 'table.' This should clarify a few things."

table

1a. An article of furniture supported by one or more vertical legs and having a flat horizontal surface. b. The objects laid out for a meal on this article of furniture. 2. The food and drink served at meals; fare: kept an excellent table. 3. The company of people assembled around a table, as for a meal. 4. Games A piece of furniture serving as a playing surface, as for faro, roulette, or dice. Often used in the plural. 5. Games a. Either of the leaves of a backgammon board. b. tables Obsolete The game of backgammon. 6. A plateau or tableland. 7a. A flat facet cut across the top of a precious stone. b. A stone or gem cut in this fashion. 8. Music a. The front part of the body of a stringed instrument. b. The sounding board of a harp. 9. Architecture a. A raised or sunken rectangular panel on a wall. b. A raised horizontal surface or continuous band on an exterior wall; a stringcourse. 10. A part of the human palm framed by four lines, analyzed in palmistry. 11. An orderly arrangement of data, especially one in which the data are arranged in columns and rows in an essentially rectangular form. 12. An abbreviated list, as of contents; a synopsis. 13. An engraved slab or tablet bearing an inscription or a device. 14. Anatomy The inner or outer flat layer of bones of the skull separated by the diploe. 15. tables A system of laws or decrees; a code: the tables of Moses.

"Did I say 'clarify'? Even more kinds of tables. Well, #11 would include my Multiplication Table as well as the standard Periodic Table. Ah #15. I have read where the Ten Commandments have been removed from schools but they are no longer on tables of stone. Next. Next."

periodic table

"Let's see how simple they can make this sound."

Chemistry A tabular arrangement of the elements according to their atomic numbers so that elements with similar properties are in the same column.

"Well. I must say, that doesn't sound nearly so complicated as I remembered it. Oh, it's getting late. 239 entries is a reasonable sample of 909. I'm going to *table* this project and check in with Holmes."

3

"Holmes, have you made any headway?"

"Indeed, Watson, my time has been well spent. And what did you find in your 'table' search?"

"The only table that was once in elementary classrooms and seems now to be missing is the Multiplication Table, apparently replaced by the calculator."

"You have an interesting mind, Watson. I would certainly have considered that an option if it weren't for an anonymous inquiry I made at the school where the professor teaches. In talking to one of his students I learned that the Professor was indeed referring to the Periodic Table of Elements."

"My God, Holmes, is the man insane?"

"You must think more deeply, Watson. This chap is saying the Periodic Table of Elements rightfully belongs to the minds of the young people in our elementary schools and that fear and ignorance in the minds of teachers and administrators has stolen it away from them."

"I can't believe you're saying this, Holmes. I think you rather agree with this Professor Bumpkin."

"I believe it's Professor Dalton. I must say I am fascinated with the notion, Watson, but it will no doubt be difficult to prove the Professor's allegation as true. Tell me, Watson, when did you start learning the alphabet?"

"The alphabet? Before I can even remember. What's your point here, Holmes?"

"When did you start learning numbers?"

"The answer is the same, Sir; before I can even remember. Come on, Holmes, is there some association you are attempting to make to the Periodic Table of Elements? If so, Sir, it is lost on me, I'm afraid."

"Watson, I want you to learn what you can before tomorrow concerning the Elements of the Periodic Table. I am calling the good Professor to set up a meeting for us as soon as possible and I want us to be ready."

"That is a tall order, my dear Holmes. All those elements are complicated, confusing and downright boring. But, I'll give it the old one-two. What will you be doing?"

"I'm going to visit my granddaughter. She is just now in the first grade. I will test my theory on her.

4

"What has happened to Holmes? He is not usually this mad. But I will humor his madness for one night. Another date with my dear computer: refdesk.com; American Heritage Dictionary; definition: elements. Oh goodie. Only 406 search results. What to do? Oh well. Here we go."

noble gas
Any of the **elements** in Group O of the periodic table, including helium, neon, argon, krypton, xenon, and radon, which are monatomic and with limited exceptions chemically...

"Hmmm. Group O? 'Helium' I recognize. 'Neon' makes signs. I don't know 'argon'. Superman was from the planet 'Krypton'. 'Xenon' is some mythical warrior. And 'radon' is something you have to watch out for in your basement. The rest is gibberish. I will press on."

transition element

Any of the metallic **elements** that have an incomplete inner electron shell and that serve as transitional links between the most and the least electropositive in a...

"My head is already spinning. I am a visual learner. I need to find a picture of this thing. But, since I'm here, I'll wade through some more babel."

nonmetal
Any of a number of **elements**, such as oxygen or sulfur, that lack the physical and chemical properties of metals....

"I knew that. Oxygen is a gas, not a metal. That's just common knowledge. I imagine a first grader even knows that one."

periodic table
Chemistry A tabular arrangement of the **elements** according to their atomic numbers so that **elements** with similar properties are in the same column.

"It sounds so simple and innocent. Why did we have such a difficult time with it in Middle School?

metal
Any of a category of electropositive **elements** that usually have a shiny surface, are generally good conductors of heat and electricity, and can be melted or fused,...

nucleosynthesis
The process by which heavier chemical **elements** are synthesized from hydrogen nuclei in the interiors of stars.

"This seems to say that all the heavier elements were produced in stars. Stars, eh? I've always wondered where the elements came from. So, I am built of star dust. Not a bad thought."

rare-earth element
Any of the abundant metallic elements of atomic number 57 through 71. Also called lanthanide. So called because they were originally thought to be rare....

alkaline-earth metal

Any of a group of metallic **elements**, especially calcium, strontium, magnesium, and barium, but generally including beryllium and radium. Also called alkaline earth....

"Ahh, calcium. Milk. Strong bones. Alkaline. Alka-Seltzer. Calcium carbonate. Antacid. There's another one I can relate to."

41) **element**
1. A fundamental, essential, or irreducible constituent of a composite entity. **2. elements** The basic assumptions or principles of a subject. **3.** *Mathematics* **a.** A member of a set. **b.** A point, line, or plane. **c.** A part of a geometric configuration, such as an angle in a triangle. **d.** The generatrix of a geometric figure. **e.** Any of the terms in the rectangular array of terms that constitute a matrix or determinant. **4.** *Chemistry & Physics* A substance composed of atoms having an identical number of protons in each nucleus. **Elements** cannot be reduced to simpler substances by normal chemical means. See table on page 578–579. **5.** One of four substances, earth, air, fire, or water, formerly regarded as a fundamental constituent of the universe. **6.** *Electricity* The resistance wire in an electrical appliance such as a heater or an oven. **7. elements** The forces that constitute the weather, especially severe or inclement weather: *outside paint that had been damaged by the elements.* **8.** An environment naturally suited to or associated with an individual: *He is in his element when traveling. The business world is her element.* **9.** A distinct group within a larger community: *the dissident element on campus.* **10.** A part of a military force, especially: **a.** A ground unit in an air force comparable to a platoon. **b.** A unit of an air force equal to two or three aircraft. **11. elements** The bread and wine of the Eucharist.

"Number 4 is very interesting: 'A substance composed of atoms...cannot be reduced to simpler substances by normal chemical means. See the table on page 578-579.' See the table? I'd love to, but I don't have a bloody book in front of me; although, a picture is beginning to take shape: a rectangular 'table' made up of columns of 'elements' according to whether it is a gas or a metal and each 'element' is made of its own identical 'atoms'."

actinide
Any of a series of chemically similar, radioactive **elements** with atomic numbers ranging from 89 (actinium) through 103 (lawrencium).

80) periodic law
Chemistry The principle that the properties of the **elements** recur periodically as their atomic numbers increase.

"I wonder what properties recur periodically? I'm sure Holmes is on to that."

Boyle, Robert
British physicist and chemist whose precise definitions of chemical **elements** and reactions began the separation of chemistry from alchemy.

"The British take the lead again. Good show, Boyle.

alkali metal
Any of a group of soft, white, low-density, low-melting, highly reactive metallic **elements**, including lithium, sodium, potassium, rubidium, cesium, and francium.

"Sodium is half of salt. Potassium has something to do with pickles! And I sadly seem to recall radioactive cesium being a pollutant from our local nuclear power plant. This list of elements reminds me of a delightful Tom Lehrer song."

neptunium
A silvery, metallic, naturally radioactive element, atomic number 93, the first of the transuranium **elements**.

heavy ion
The nucleus of a heavy element. When such nuclei are caused to collide at high velocities, new **elements** are created.

"Does this mean that elements are still being created? If so, the Periodic Table is not complete. Much like the rest of life, always in process; never finished, even in death. Hmmm.

halogen
Any of a group of five chemically related nonmetallic **elements** including fluorine, chlorine, bromine, iodine, and astatine.

"I know 'fluorine' from fluoride in toothpaste. And 'chlorine' is the other half of salt and can somehow sterilize water for drinking. We get 'iodine' in iodized salt to prevent goiter. But the other two I don't know. I rather enjoy this when I find something to which I can relate."

periodicity
1. The quality or state of being periodic; recurrence at regular intervals. **2.** The repetition of similar properties in chemical **elements**, as indicated by their positioning in the periodic table.

"I'm sure women are keen to periodicity. 'Repetition of similar properties' makes me think of the *halogens*. They are probably all in the same column."

alphabet
1. The letters of a language, arranged in the order fixed by custom. **2.** A system of characters or symbols representing sounds or things. **3.** A set of basic parts or **elements**: *"genetic markers . . . that contain repeated sequences of the DNA alphabet"* (Sandra Blakeslee, *New York Times* 9/13/94).

"Holmes asked me when I was first taught the alphabet. The *letters* of the *alphabet* are *elements*. The *elements* of the *Periodic Table* are like *letters* of the *alphabet*. I wonder why don't we teach the Periodic Table to children like we teach the Alphabet? Wait! What am I saying? This is a trick. Holmes has tricked me into thinking like him. I should have known what he was up to."

oxygen

Symbol O A nonmetallic element constituting 21 percent of the atmosphere by volume that occurs as a diatomic gas, O2, and in many compounds.

"Only 21 percent? What is the rest of the atmosphere composed of? No wonder I get out of breath exercising. There's hardly any oxygen in the bloody atmosphere. I can't do any more tonight. Limited oxygen I'll tell him. Something has been stolen all right, Holmes has stolen my good judgment. Maybe tomorrow I'll get my own mind back."

5

"Well, Holmes, you must be quite proud of yourself, tricking me that way."

"Whatever do you mean, my dear Watson?"

"I mean getting me to think like you by sending me to research 'elements'. I'm on to you, Holmes. I'm no dummy, you know."

"You are a thoughtful man, Watson, and I am proud of *you*, not me. Evidently you have had a great evolution in your thinking. Are you ready to meet the Professor?"

"How do you always seem to turn things around, Holmes? Yes, yes, I'm ready to meet the dear Professor Bumpkin or Dalton."

"Good. He is in the next room waiting for us."

"Holmes!?!"

"Professor Dalton, may I introduce Dr. Watson, my friend and colleague of many years."

"My pleasure indeed. Any relation to the Watson of Watson and Crick?"

"Probably distant cousins, as are we all; but not a close relation. And are you related to the famous chemist, John Dalton?"

"As you said so well, probably distant cousins."

"Well Professor, Watson informed me of the Times article concerning your allegation that the Periodic Table is missing from elementary schools throughout the country, implying it has been stolen. I must say that is quite an accusation."

"I'm sure it is widely misunderstood. A newspaper article can hardly do justice to what I am actually alleging. You see, I believe that fear and ignorance in the minds of school teachers and administrators has stolen the Periodic Table away from the very children to whom such basic information rightfully belongs."

"Seems as though I heard that idea expressed by someone else not too long ago. Didn't you say something to that effect, Holmes?"

"I was merely sharing with you, Watson, what Professor Dalton's young student had expressed to me. It fascinated me immediately and I knew we must meet and discuss it with you, Dalton. How long have you been on to this idea?"

"It evolved in my teaching sometime during the 1990s. I can't actually recall the moment, but once it was in my mind, there was no turning back. Tell me Holmes, Watson, what would you say are the 5 elements of the periodic table that we should be teaching children in the 1st grade?"

"How can you teach anything so complicated as the Periodic Table to first-graders?"

"Tell me Watson, don't first-graders breath, eat, and drink the very same elements that we adults do?"

"I never thought about breathing, eating, and drinking elements."

"That's exactly my point, Watson. Children do these very same things so why not tell them what they are breathing, eating, and drinking? It is not so complicated to a child that they breath *oxygen* and drink H-two-O. H is for *hydrogen*. There, they already have two elements on the periodic table and we're just breathing air and drinking water."

"I see your method, Dalton. You're taking something already familiar to the student and attaching a name and identifying symbol to it; then, inserting it on to a numbered chart that we call the

Periodic Table. Very well done. You've given us two elements; may I suggest a third?"

"It should not be difficult for you, Holmes, with the statements we've already made. You may give all three."

"In the area of eating, we all need carbohydrates in some amount and carbohydrates are the combination of carbon dioxide and water formed during photosynthesis. Therefore, I postulate the third element to be *carbon*."

"No first grader knows about photosynthesis, Holmes. You're already way over their heads."

"But my dear Watson, they all do eat carbohydrates. It is simply the teachers job to associate carbon with carbohydrates and the child will easily accept that fact. You accepted two plus two equaling four long before you actually understood the concept of addition."

"Uncle! But two can play this little game. You are not the only one here who can make good guesses. I will offer another element myself. I suggest *fluorine*."

"Excellent, Watson. I see exactly where you are going. Your refresher on the elements must have produced a worthy yield. Most children brush their teeth with a fluoride tooth paste to prevent cavities. Are we correct, Dalton?"

"You couldn't be more on target. This is actually quite exciting hearing you two process these ideas. It reinforces to me that I am not some kind of whacko from outer space. I truly believe that once teachers see how easy this is, they will love using it."

"So, Professor Dalton, you've given two and we each determined one. What is your fifth element?"

"What do you think, Holmes?"

"I must say my mind is racing so fast now that I'm already up to eleven elements at the very least. It is difficult to settle for just one, but, I will propose, that since all children eat protein as well as fat and carbohydrate, and that protein contains one element beyond carbon, hydrogen, and oxygen, your fifth element must be *nitrogen*."

"Holmes, you chaps have convinced me that first graders might actually grasp oxygen, hydrogen, carbon, and fluorine, but how are they going to relate to nitrogen?"

"I wasn't sure myself, Watson, until I talked with my granddaughter yesterday. As you recall, she is in the 1st grade. We were sitting at the dinner table after supper and I commented about the variety of objects on the table. That led to the game of 'name the table' and we went around the house naming all the different kinds of tables."

"Like coffee table and end table?"

"Yes, and they even have a pool table and a ping-pong table in their basement. Then I told her, when I was in 1st grade, we used writing tablets or little tables on which to write our lessons. I believe some schools still use the term."

"I should invite you to my classroom, Holmes, you are a master teacher. What association did you build on next?"

"I drew a box with 10 rows and 10 columns. She helped me greatly in filling in all the numbers, 1 to 100. I told her we had just made a different kind of table, a table of numbers."

"Do 1st graders know all their numbers?"

"Most do, Watson, and the ones that don't seem to catch on quickly with repetition. At this point I broached the concept of 'elements' by asking what made up a family? She obliged by offering a lengthy list including the family cat. I simply said all those items she had mentioned were elements of her family."

"Most children have very short attention spans, Holmes. The poor girl must have been wanting to go play by now."

"Not at all, Watson. You see, we were playing already. Everything we were doing was like a game and she was a most enthusiastic player. At this point I asked her if I might have a glass of water. When she returned, I asked her what elements made up water."

"I'll wager she had no idea at all."

"You are almost correct, Watson, until I rephrased the question: 'Do you know another name for water?' And with the assurance of Eleanor Roosevelt she said, H-2-O. And as shivers went up and down my body, I said, H is for hydrogen and O is for oxygen. It was indeed an evolutionary moment."

"Observations, explorations, framing and reframing knowledge, games, associations, rephrasing questions. Holmes, you have a marvelous tool-kit for teaching. I hope you don't mind my taking notes?"

"Not at all, dear man, I'm sure you do the same in your classroom. By the way, when I said 'oxygen' she said, 'That's the good air we breathe in and carbon dioxide is the bad air we breathe out.' That was totally unexpected and yet it seemed so common for her to speak it. We now had three elements for the Periodic Table of which I crudely drew a facsimile with lines only."

"So, you actually started placing elements on the table?"

"Yes, Watson. It felt like the natural thing to do and she felt like we were starting another game. We walked over to a large philodendron next to a window and talked a bit about people breathing and plants breathing. I was building another bridge that I wasn't sure she would be able to cross. I truly had never talked like this to a child and, quite frankly, I was in awe."

"Well, did she get across the bridge or not, Holmes. Come on, man, don't keep us in suspense."

"I asked her if there were any plants that she ate and we were instantly off on another exploration, first of the refrigerator and then to the family garden in the back yard by moonlight. Well moonlight led to talking about sunlight and energy and plants and people. Soon I was feeling like an old story teller and she was in my lap not far from her bedtime."

"But nitrogen. You didn't get to nitrogen, Holmes."

"Watson, it had been an adventure with this young person that I shall never forget. And above all, I believe I gained a respect for young people that I had never had before that night. They are bright, eager, inquisitive, fun, energetic, and I must say, inspiring. Nitrogen, Watson? Nitrogen would be no problem, I had no doubt."

"And now you have my mind racing, Holmes. How can we get this kind of interaction into our country's classrooms? It would be so natural for our young people. Elements would just be a part of their common language and they could visualize them in their place on the Table as they placed them there, one-by-one."

"I agree that the challenge lies not with the first-graders, but with teachers and administrators. They have so many obligations to fulfill, I'm sure they shun the thought of adding one more thing."

"But it would take so little time and it would flow into so many subjects: nutrition, energy, geology, the environment, ecology, mathematics, global warming, all the sciences, and even history and language arts. With the smallest investment, the rewards would be enormous."

"You don't have to convince me, Dalton. I am a believer. And the teachers and administrators will become believers in due time. Change is often fearful to some, but change is the most consistent law of the universe. Have confidence that they will be receptive to the message when heard in the proper context."

"How can you be so certain, Sir?"

"Holmes, let me try and answer that by asking Watson a question. We observe that all life, as we know it, has DNA to replicate it. All DNA is made up of only five elements. Can you name the five elements, Watson?"

"I'm sure I could make a few good guesses, but, frankly, I have never thought about it. Go ahead, Holmes, you tell him the five elements in DNA."

"Well, Watson, that would be hydrogen, oxygen, carbon, nitrogen, and phosphorus."

"Holmes, how did you know that?"

"It's elementary, my dear Watson."

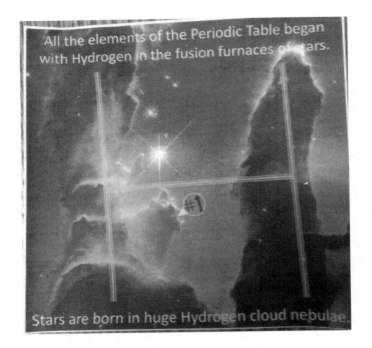

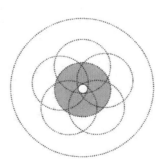

About the Author

Identity & Anonymity: An Artful Anthology (2016)
by Jonathan Talbot, Leslie Fandrich, and Steven M. Specht
Page 111

RICHARD B. DALTON

If it is to be, it is up to US!

I am not my body, nor my beliefs;
but an observant, willful soul, thankful for the Source within All.

My 5-billion-year-old atoms, gypsies of star dust,
are having quite a journey exploring time and space.

People only observe my habits
and whatever else gets acted out
through playful, soulful expressions.

My now-tamed merchant memes
started their machinations the moment my Mom first held me.

As a biased artist of social change,
I gently draw a world, that operates on love, into being.

I honor guardians of nature,
messages of wonder, healers of misery and architects of peace.

Love excites and amuses my muse, my senses,
my inner crew, my spirit guides and soul seers everywhere.

In gratitude for the past,
in service to the present,
in responsibility for the future,
I give my life.

Richard B "Dick" Dalton, Co-Creator at Value Life Associates, is 72 years into his Quest.
His collage includes 35 years teaching 20,000 HBCU students as a PhD Health Educator
and Life Coach. Other hats he wears or has worn include husband, father, actor,
minister, singer/songwriter, Social Artist, playwright, philosopher, editor, hitch-hiker,
hospital corpsman, war resister/peace advocate, and author. Twitter @daltondster.
https://www.capitalcityproductions.org/actor---dick-dalton-bio.html

Acknowledgements

From Raul saving my life at the quarry as a youngster to Kandy helping in the cover design, many people have been acknowledged for their role in making this book what it is. I have a few more to mention.

On a Renaissance trip to Greece in 2015, Jean Houston and Mark Posner offered helpful feedback on an early rendition of the book. At a Social Artistry Conference in 2016, Phil Johncock gently 'cracked the whip' and guided the book to its manifestation on Amazon Kindle.

Fernando Manrique Florindez dialogued with me while reading a draft during a Deep Travel tour in Morocco; his critique was constructive and affirming. The two tour leaders, Christina Ammon (reading the Kindle version) and Dot Fisher-Smith (scanning the draft for paperback), gave confirmation and encouragement.

Back home I've had extended conversations about the book with Tom Durkin, Jim Dyke, and Joni Weinbaum. Their constant love and support carries me on.

Thirty years of students at Lincoln University contributed in so many ways to the ideas and expressions used in the book. Likewise, my colleagues in the ministry helped hone several of the tools offered here. My community theatre family in Jefferson City—a grand lot all—get my salute; your names are on all the marques.

Throughout all, my wife Marsha has been my chief cheerleader and sometimes proof reader/sounding board. We have discussed, agreed, disagreed, and continue to maintain our loving partnership. My daughter Alethea gave excellent generational advice that helped guide key aspects of my presentation.

I bow and give thanks to the Earth and the Great Mystery that muse and amuse us with connections, visions, lines of thought, coincidences, hunches, and the power to overcome and press on through the storm. I see them in all things—in each person, plant, critter, and sunrise. I reach out with gratitude, knowing the possibilities put forth in this book are for every individual.

Made in the USA
Lexington, KY
03 October 2017